THE CHURCH OF GOD IN CHRIST
PRESIDING BISHOP

Bishop J. Drew Sheard

"UNFINISHED BUSINESS"

"Jesus saith unto them, My meat is to do the will of him that sent me, and to finish his work." John 4:34, KJV

Evangelist Terri Hannett • Executive Director
Supervisor Barachias Irons • Chief Editor

**Church Of
God In Christ**
PUBLISHING HOUSE

806 East Brooks Road, Memphis, Tennessee 38116
P. O. Box 161330, Memphis, Tennessee 38186
• **Toll Free:** 1-877-746-8578 | Fax: 901-743-1555
• **Website:** www.cogicpublishinghouse.net
• **Email:** sales@cogicpublishinghouse.net

Greetings in the name of our Lord and Savior, Jesus Christ.

In this time of rapid change, it is vitally important for blood washed individuals to actively participate in our churches and communities to assure our voices are heard and God is glorified.

We must remain "steadfast, unmovable, always abounding in the work of the Lord, forasmuch as ye know that your labor is not in vain in the Lord".

With that being said, I want you to know, we have "Unfinished Business" in upholding our Christian duties and engaging in constructive dialogue to address societal challenges and the continued advancement of the Kingdom of God.

The Power for Living curriculum is filled with scriptures that will encourage and motivate you to keep pressing your way in the things of the Lord.

I encourage you to share the Word of God on every occasion and live so God can use you, anywhere and anytime.

Sincerely,

J. Drew Sheard,

Presiding Bishop and Chief Apostle

Church Of God In Christ, Inc.

CHURCH OF GOD IN CHRIST, INC.
930 Mason St. | Memphis, TN 98126
Office: 901.947.9300 | Fax: 901.947.9327
www.COGIC.org

THE VOICE OF THE CHAIRMAN
OF THE PUBLISHING BOARD

Blessings in the name of the Lord Jesus Christ,

The fact that you are reading this letter indicates that God has blessed you to experience another year of His grace and mercy. We often transition from one season to the next and sometimes take for granted the privilege God affords us to see a new year, a new season, and a new day. Thank God for our now and our next!

Our Presiding Bishop has ushered us into a new season this year, realizing that our church has "Unfinished Business." In John 4:34, Jesus, speaking to disciples, said, "My meat is to do the will of him that sent me, and to finish his work." Here, Jesus reminds his disciples of the purpose of their mission and that both planting spiritual seeds and collecting the harvest are valuable. And God wants us to know that if we expect to reap a harvest, we must first scatter the seed of the Good News of Christ to a dying and depleted world.

Understand that the seed has no flaws because it is God's Word. It holds much potential, but it can only be activated if it takes root in fertile soil. Our job as the church is to plant the seed of life into the heart of every person: "Go ye into all the world and preach the gospel to every creature" (Mark 16:15). Once these seeds are planted, our churches will grow: "The harvest truly is plenteous, but the labourers are few" (Matthew 9:37).

Sunday School is the foundational building block of our church. God's seed is cultivated during school on Sunday so we can face the world on Monday. We have an obligation to spread God's word so that His business may be accomplished here on earth.

I thank the thousands of loyal supporters of our literature who partner in God's mission of sharing the Good News to the world. We have work to do! I want to personally thank you for answering the call so that lives may be changed and transformed.

We are also in a time of political change. So, I ask that you continue to pray for the unity of our country and pray for God to manifest Himself in our lives and our churches in a new way. I ask that the Lord shift the winds of grace and favor in our direction so that we can experience Him as we have never experienced Him before. Church, let's do the work. We have unfinished business!

In His Service,
Bishop Uleses C. Henderson, Jr.
Chairman of the Publishing Board
Church Of God In Christ Inc.

THE VOICE OF MARKETING

Dear Saints,

Greetings in the matchless name of our Lord and Savior, Jesus Christ! I pray this letter finds you in good health and strengthened by God's unchanging grace. As we approach another season of celebration and reflection, I am reminded of God's faithfulness and His call to us to remain steadfast in the work of the Kingdom.

The theme for this year, **"Unfinished Business,"** compels us to look inward and upward as we commit ourselves to fulfilling the divine mandate given to each of us. Jesus reminds us in John 4:34, *"My food is to do the will of Him who sent Me, and to finish His work."* Just as our Savior found sustenance in obedience to God's purpose, so too must we press forward to complete the assignments He entrusted us.

In these challenging times, it is easy to grow weary or become distracted by the cares of life. Yet, the work of the Kingdom cannot wait. There are souls to save, broken hearts to mend, and communities to uplift. The business of love, justice, mercy, and evangelism remains unfinished, and God has chosen us—His Church—as vessels to carry out His will.

This is a clarion call to all of us:
- **To stay mission-minded** in advancing the Gospel.
- **To serve tirelessly** in our communities and congregations.
- **To build bridges of hope** where there is despair.
- **To finish the race** with the confidence that we have done the work He sent us to do.

Let us approach this season with renewed passion and unwavering faith. As we labor together, may we keep our eyes on the One who is the Author and Finisher of our faith.

I encourage you, beloved saints, to recommit yourselves to the work God has placed in your hands. Whether in your local church, family, or community, know your labor is not in vain. The harvest is plentiful, and the time to finish the work is now.

May the Holy Spirit empower us to persevere and complete the mission with joy and diligence. Thank you for your faithful service, your prayers, and your love for the body of Christ. Together, let us press forward, confident in the promise that He who began a good work in us will bring it to completion.

With great expectation for what God will do in and through us,

Yours in Christ,

Sandra S. Jones, B.S., MTh., PhD (c)
Chairman of Marketing (Board)
Senior Marketing/Sales Consultant
Church Of God In Christ Publishing House

QUARTERLY QUIZ

The questions on this page may be used in several ways: as a pretest at the beginning of the quarter; as a review at the end of the quarter; or as a review after each lesson. The questions are based on the Scripture text of each lesson (King James Version).

LESSON 1

1. What did John see happening to Jesus that caused him to marvel at His presence (John 1:32)?

_____

_____

2. Complete the following Scripture from John 1:34, "And I saw, and _____ _____ that this is the _____ _____ _____."

_____

_____

LESSON 2

1. Name two characteristics (or titles) that John lists about the Holy Spirit in John 14:16–17.

_____

_____

2. If a believer_____Jesus, then what will happen according to John 14:23?

_____

_____

LESSON 3

1. After Jesus spoke with the disciples, what is their response to His departure (John 16:6)?

_____

_____

2. If Jesus does not leave the disciples, who will not be able to come and guide them (John 16:7)?

_____

_____

LESSON 4

1. Define the word "remit" in John 20:23.

2. Jesus showed the disciples His _____ and _____ (John 20:20).

_____

_____

LESSON 5

1. Believers should not be like _____ because he was with the "evil one," and he _____ his brother (1 John 3:12).

_____

_____

2. Paul tells the believers that they are to love through _____ and _____ _____ (1 John 3:18).

LESSON 6

1. We love God because

_____

_____(1 John

4:19).

2. If a person claims to love God, but hates his brother, then the person is a _____ (1 John 4:20).

LESSON 7

1. What type of animal did Jesus ask two disciples bring to Him (Mark 11:7)?

_____

_____

2. Jesus came into_____ and went into the _____ (Mark 11:11).

_____

_____

LESSON 8

1. Who has risen from the dead and has become the firstfruits for those who have fallen asleep (1 Corinthians 15:20)?

_____

_____

2. In Adam, all men died, but Christ makes all what (1 Corinthians 15:22)?

_____

_____

LESSON 9

1. John greets people with _____, _____, and _____ (2 John 3).

_____

_____

2. And now, _____ _____, I am not writing you a _____ _____ but one we have had from the beginning. I ask that _____ _____ _____ _____ (2 John 5).

_____

_____

LESSON 10

1. Who does John say has arrogant and unhospitable behavior (3 John 9–10)?

_____

_____

2. John encourages believers to _____ _____ because it is of God and not to do evil (3 John 11).

_____

_____

LESSON 11

1. Paul does not want the Corinthians to be _____ in their understanding (**1 Corinthians 12:1**).

_____

_____

2. List some of the gifts that Paul shares that are from the Spirit (**1 Corinthians 12:10**).

_____

_____

LESSON 12

1. Is the body made up of one member or many (**1 Corinthians 12:14**)?

_____

_____

2. How does Paul convey his point of the body of the church as one (**1 Corinthians 12:16**)?

_____

_____

LESSON 13

1. Though I speak with the _____ _____ and of angels, and have not_____ I am become as sounding brass, or a tinkling cymbal. (**1 Corinthians 13:1**).

_____

_____

2. Paul "gains nothing" if he does not have _____ (**1 Corinthians 13:3**).

_____

_____

ADULT QUARTERLY

SPRING QUARTER 2025

MARCH • APRIL • MAY

Unit 1 • The Pledge of God's Presence

MARCH

Unit 2 • The Community of the Beloved Disciple

APRIL

Unit 3 • One in the Bond of Love

MAY

THE WORD OF GOD

BIBLE BASIS: John 1:29–34

BIBLE TRUTH: John testifies that the baptism of the Holy Spirit surpasses water baptism and that the Spirit surpasses water baptism and that the Spirit bears witness that Jesus is God the Son.

MEMORY VERSE: "And I saw, and bare record that this is the Son of God" (John 1:34).

LESSON AIM: By the end of the lesson, your students will: EXPLORE John's account of Jesus' baptism, RELIVE emotions felt while observing or participating in a baptism; and ASSESS how Christians live out their baptismal covenant.

BIBLE BACKGROUND: John 1:29–34; Joel 2:23–27—Read and incorporate the insights gained from the Background Scriptures into your study of the lesson.

LESSON SCRIPTURE

JOHN 1:29–34, KJV

29 The next day John seeth Jesus coming unto him, and saith, Behold the Lamb of God, which taketh away the sin of the world.

30 This is he of whom I said, After me cometh a man which is preferred before me: for he was before me.

31 And I knew him not: but that he should be made manifest to Israel, therefore am I come baptizing with water.

32 And John bare record, saying, I saw the Spirit descending from heaven like a dove, and it abode upon him.

33 And I knew him not: but he that sent me to baptize with water, the same said unto me, Upon whom thou shalt see the Spirit descending, and remaining on him, the same is he which baptizeth with the Holy Ghost.

34 And I saw, and bare record that this is the Son of God.

BIBLICAL DEFINITIONS

A. Baptize (John 1:31, 33) *baptizo* (Gk.)—To dip repeatedly, to immerse, to submerge.

B. Bear record (vv. 32, 34) *martureo* (Gk.)—To affirm that one has seen or heard or experienced something, to testify.

LIFE NEED FOR TODAY'S LESSON

AIM: Students will develop a closer relationship with Christ and discern the many competing religious and political values in the world.

INTRODUCTION

John the Baptist—A Holy Man

John the Baptist was a Nazarite, the son of Zacharias, the priest and Elisabeth. His birth was foretold by the angel Gabriel. Gabriel told Zacharias and Elisabeth of John's birth and explained that he would be "great in the eyes of the Lord" and would be "filled with the Holy Ghost" (**Luke 1:15**). He was meant to lead many Israelites to the Lord and would prepare them for the coming of the Messiah. Gabriel also gave instructions that their son was never to drink wine or hard liquor, and that they should name him John. This news was surprising to Zacharias and Elisabeth, because they were very old and Elisabeth wasn't able to have children. Their baby was born, strong in the Spirit just as Gabriel had said. Prior to beginning his ministry in Israel, John lived in the Judean wilderness, between Jerusalem and the Dead Sea. Other accounts about John in the Gospels indicate that he wore camel hair and a leather belt, and ate locusts and honey (**Mark 1:6**). He lived in the wilderness until he began his ministry in Israel, around 26 or 27 A.D. John's ministry focused on calling for repentance, administering baptism, and prophesying about the coming Messiah. John's speaking style was bold and fearless. He urged people to confess their sins and repent. He was also critical of sin in the lives of local religious and political leaders. Shortly after bearing witness to Christ's arrival, John was imprisoned by Herod and beheaded. Jesus refers to John's witness and ministry in **John 5:35**, saying that "he was a burning and shining light."

BIBLE LEARNING

AIM: Students will testify to the power of the Spirit that Jesus is God's Son.

I. JOHN ANNOUNCES CHRIST'S ARRIVAL (John 1:29–31)

John presents Jesus as the "Lamb of God." The phrase alludes to the image of the sacrificial Passover lamb. More specifically, the phrase points to the redemptive nature of Christ's sacrifice. Animals were regularly used in Judaism as a sacrifice to cleanse sin. While the sacrifice of animals was an ongoing, repetitive process, John announces that Christ's atoning sacrifice would be a permanent solution. Furthermore, Christ's redemptive work is for everyone.

The Lamb of God (verses 29–31)

29 The next day John seeth Jesus coming unto him, and saith, Behold the Lamb of God, which taketh away the sin of the world.

As Jesus approached John, John saw something, a sign, that affirmed the identity of the One John was paving the way for. The Lamb of God, being divine, would take away the sin of the whole world. Jesus was the sacrificial Lamb who offered Himself without spot to God (**Hebrews 9:24–28**). The word for "taketh away" is *airo* (Gk., **EYE-row**), which means to take away, bear away, or carry off. It was language that would remind the listeners of Yom Kippur, the Day of Atonement, in which the scapegoat would be set loose into the wilderness to carry off the sin of the nation (**Leviticus 16:20–22**). The language here in John suggests that Jesus is not only the Passover Lamb, serving as a reminder of God's protection of His people in Egypt (**Exodus 12**), but that He is also an atoning sacrifice, accomplishing more than a normal Passover lamb ever could.

30 This is he of whom I said, After me cometh a man which is preferred before me; for he was before me.

John points out that Jesus is the One whom he was referring to in **verse 27**. He also adds that Jesus is "preferred before" (Gk. *emprosthen*, **EM-prohs-thehn**) John in rank, because He existed "before" (Gk. *protos*, **PRO-toss**) John in time. John is speaking of Christ as the eternal Word who existed before creation. This is the basis of Christ's ranking above John. As the pre-incarnate Christ, Jesus will always be superior to every created thing because He is the Creator (**John 1:1–3**).

31 And I knew him not; but that he should be made manifest to Israel, therefore am I come baptizing with water.

John did not know the identity of the Christ, but that did not prevent him from carrying out his duty to baptize. He knew that through his ministry, the Christ would be "manifest" to Israel. The word "manifest" (Gk. *phanero*, **fah-neigh-RAH-oh**) means more than just to appear. One may appear in a false identity, but to be made manifest is to appear as one truly is. This is significant because Jesus assumed the identity of an everyday Jewish man. Now His true identity would be revealed.

QUESTION 1

How do you think it felt for John to finally be able to declare Jesus' identity to everyone (John 1:29–30)?

II. JESUS IS THE SON OF GOD (vv. 32–34)

Here John is reflecting on an event that is recorded in **Matthew 3:13–17, Mark 1:9–11,** and **Luke 3:21–22.** Jesus went to John to be baptized in the Jordan River. While John was baptizing Jesus, he witnessed the Holy Spirit rest on Jesus in the form of a dove. This event was significant, not only because of its spectacular nature, but because John had been told that this sign would mark the man who would baptize with the Holy Spirit. John clearly indicates God's direction in his baptism ministry and his testimony to Jesus' identity. God instructed him to baptize to prepare the people for Jesus' arrival.

The Spirit, Like a Dove (verses 32–34)

32 And John bare record, saying, I saw the Spirit descending from heaven like a dove, and it abode upon him.

This was the sign by which John was told he would know the identity of the Christ. We do not know whether it was an actual dove or if the emphasis is on the manner of the Spirit's descension. That is, it could be that John is describing the way in which the Spirit came down and hovered over Jesus. Doves were associated with God in various way in Jewish tradition. A dove was used to let Noah know when the water had receded enough to reveal dry land (**Genesis 8**). They also announce God's presence (**Isaiah 60:8; Psalm 68:13**).

33 And I knew him not; but he that sent me to baptize with water, the same said unto me, Upon whom thou shalt see the Spirit descending, and remaining on him, the same is he which baptizeth with the Holy Ghost.

John did not know who the Son of God would be. This does not mean that John did not know Jesus. John and Jesus were cousins, but John did not know that Jesus was the Christ, the one whom God would send after him. The Lord instructed John to baptize and look for the sign of the Spirit descending as the indicator of the Messiah's identity. John affirms that Jesus came to do more than baptize with water: He came to baptize with the Holy Spirit.

34 And I saw, and bare record that this is the Son of God.

In this concluding sentence of John the Baptist's testimony, John affirmed that he was an eyewitness to that which he had spoken. This language is from court language when testifying. All that John did not know before was made plain by the sign, and John knew that Jesus is the Son of God. This could only be known through revelation given by God.

QUESTION 2

John states that the Holy Spirit remained on Jesus. What is the significance of this distinction (**v. 33**)?

11

BIBLE APPLICATION

AIM: Students will experience a stirring in their hearts, mind, and spirit when they testify to who Christ is.

People still "bear witness" today. Have you ever asked someone to provide you with a reference or letter of recommendation for a new job? Or maybe a former colleague has asked if you would share your experience of how they performed as a worker. These are modern-day examples of testifying to someone's identity or character. The Holy Spirit within each believer testifies to the fact that we are God's children (**Romans 8:16**). As His children, we have been charged with witnessing to the power and person of Christ. We are meant to be living recommendations of Christ's love.

STUDENTS' RESPONSES

AIM: Students will seek to live consistently with the covenant made at baptism.

John the Baptist provided witness testimony to the identity of Jesus as the Son of God and the redemptive sacrifice for the sins of humanity. Consider ways in which you could testify to the person of Christ this week. Ask God to reveal opportunities to share the love of Christ with your family, friends, and coworkers.

If you don't feel like you're a very reliable witness to the person and ministry of Christ, ask God what changes you can make in your life. Ask the Holy Spirit to give you strength to make those changes in your life.

PRAYER

Dear Lord, we are blessed to experience a wonderful baptism in Jesus as we stay connected to You through the Holy Spirit. Bless us and keep us as we witness to others about the goodness and transforming power of Jesus in our lives. In Jesus' Name we pray. Amen.

DIG A LITTLE DEEPER

The concept of "baptism" in the New Testament is sometimes made more complex than it has to be in the Church. We get clarity when we consider the meaning of the word in Greek, and carefully examine the Scriptures for the examples of baptism. Baptizo means "to dip or sink" and was used among the Greeks to signify the dyeing of a garment. The image of an artisan immersing material into dye to change its color is instructional for us. Baptism in the New Testament similarly always involves a baptizer and a medium into which we are baptized.

There are three baptisms in a believer's life: 1) the Holy Spirit baptizes us into Christ (or into the Church); 2) Jesus baptizes us into the Holy Spirit; 3) the Church baptizes us in water. The first baptism occurs when we come to saving faith in Jesus Christ. The Holy Spirit effectively dips us into the blood of Jesus, and we become new creations. We instantly become members of the Church invisible. This is what the apostle Paul referred to when he wrote that there is "one Lord, one faith, one baptism" (Eph. 4:5; also consider 1 Cor. 12:13 and Gal. 3:27). Subsequent to salvation, the baptism in the Holy Ghost is available to believers who ask for it. John the Baptist informed us that Jesus would perform this baptism for his people (Mat. 3:11; Mark 1:8; Luke 3:16; John 1:33); it is designed to give us the power to be Christ's witnesses on the earth (Acts 1:8). The third baptism is performed by other believers into water. This command was for all believers (Mat. 28:19). It represents obedience to Christ and openly testifies of our death to sin and resurrection to new life.

Peruse the book of Acts, and you will see that most of the conversions described in detail mention all three baptisms. For example, consider the description of Philip evangelizing the city of Samaria. When the people "believed Philip preaching the things concerning the kingdom of God, and the name of Jesus Christ," that represented their baptism into Christ; then "they were baptized, both men and women," which is a reference to Philip performing water baptism (Acts 8:12). Later, when Peter and John learned of the extent of Philip's ministry to the new believers, they also labored to impart the baptism in the Holy Ghost (Acts 8:14,15). The early church desired all three baptisms for each new convert.

Ref.: Vine, William Edwy. Vine's concise dictionary of the Bible. Nashville: Nelson Reference & Electronic, 2005.

HOW TO SAY IT

Nazirite.   **NA**-ze-rite.

Bethabara.   Beth-a-**BA**-ra.

Esaias.   Es-**I**-as.

DAILY HOME BIBLE READINGS

MONDAY
The Spirit and Joseph
(Genesis 41:38–43)

TUESDAY
The Spirit and Bezalel
(Exodus 31:1–6)

WEDNESDAY
The Spirit and the Elders
(Numbers 11:11–25)

THURSDAY
Would That All Had the Spirit!
(Numbers 11:26–30)

FRIDAY
Make the Way Straight
(John 1:19–23)

SATURDAY
Why are You Baptizing?
(John 1:24–28)

SUNDAY
I Saw the Spirit Descending
(John 1:29–34)

PREPARE FOR NEXT SUNDAY

Read John 14:15–26 and study "Jesus Promises an Advocate."

Sources:
Alexander, David, and Pat Alexander. *Zondervan Handbook to the Bible*. Grand Rapids, MI: Zondervan, 1999. 240–241.
Barker, Kenneth L. and Kohlenberger III, John R., eds. *The Expositor's Bible Commentary*. Abridged Edition: New Testament. Grand Rapids, MI:
Zondervan, 1994. 299–300.
Butler, Trent C., ed. "John the Baptist." *Holman Bible Dictionary*. Electronic Edition, Quickverse. Nashville, TN: Holman Bible Publishers, 1991.
Butler, Trent C., ed. "Passover." *Holman Bible Dictionary*. Electronic Edition, Quickverse. Nashville, TN: Holman Bible Publishers, 1991.
Easton, M. G. "John the Baptist." *Easton's Bible Dictionary*. 1st ed. Oklahoma City, OK: Ellis Enterprises, 1993.

Elwell, Walter A. and Robert W. Yarbrough. *Encountering the New Testament: A Historical and Theological Survey.* Grand Rapids, MI: Baker Books, 1998. 42–43.

McGrath, Allister E. and James I. Packer, eds. *Zondervan Handbook of Christian Beliefs.* Grand Rapids, MI: Zondervan, 2005. 240–241.

Thayer, Joseph. "Baptizo." *Thayer's Greek Definitions.* 3rd ed. Electronic Edition, Quickverse. El Cajon, CA: Institute for Creation Research, 1999.

Thayer, Joseph. "Martureo." *Thayer's Greek Definitions.* 3rd ed. Electronic Edition, Quickverse. El Cajon, CA: Institute for Creation Research, 1999.

Walvoord, John F. and Roy B. Zuck, eds. *The Bible Knowledge Commentary: An Exposition of the Scriptures.* Wheaton, IL: Victor Books, 1983. 274–275.

COMMENTS / NOTES:

JESUS PROMISES AN ADVOCATE

BIBLE BASIS: John 14:15–26

BIBLE TRUTH: Jesus said that He would send the Holy Spirit to help His followers to love God and live according to God's commandments.

MEMORY VERSE: "But the Comforter, which is the Holy Ghost, whom the Father will send in my name, he shall teach you all things, and bring all things to your remembrance, whatsoever I have said unto you" (John 14:26).

LESSON AIM: By the end of the lesson, your students will: understand the significance of the Holy Spirit; recognize the power available through the Holy Spirit; and pray for the guidance of the Holy Spirit in making decisions.

BIBLE BACKGROUND: John 14:15–26; Psalm 23—Read and incorporate the insights gained from the Background Scriptures into your study of the lesson.

LESSON SCRIPTURE

JOHN 14:15–26, KJV

15 If ye love me, keep my commandments.

16 And I will pray the Father, and he shall give you another Comforter, that he may abide with you for ever;

17 Even the Spirit of truth; whom the world cannot receive, because it seeth him not, neither knoweth him: but ye know him; for he dwelleth with you, and shall be in you.

18 I will not leave you comfortless: I will come to you.

19 Yet a little while, and the world seeth me no more; but ye see me: because I live, ye shall live also.

20 At that day ye shall know that I am in my Father, and ye in me, and I in you.

21 He that hath my commandments, and keepeth them, he it is that loveth me: and he that loveth me shall be loved of my Father, and I will love him, and will manifest myself to him.

22 Judas saith unto him, not Iscariot, Lord, how is it that thou wilt manifest thyself unto us, and not unto the world?

23 Jesus answered and said unto him, If a man love me, he will keep my words: and my Father will love him, and we will come unto him, and make our abode with him.

24 He that loveth me not keepeth not my sayings: and the word which ye hear is not mine, but the Father's which sent me.

25 These things have I spoken unto you, being yet present with you.

26 But the Comforter, which is the Holy Ghost, whom the Father will send in my name, he shall teach you all things, and bring all things to your remembrance, whatsoever I have said unto you.

BIBLICAL DEFINITIONS

A. Commandments (John 14:15, 21) *entole* (Gk.)—Orders, commands, charges, precepts, injunctions.

B. Comforter (v. 16) *parakletos*

(Gk.)—One who is called to one's side, especially called to one's aid; one who pleads another's cause before a judge.

LIFE NEED FOR TODAY'S LESSON

AIM: Students will know what is right, but struggle to follow through as they should.

INTRODUCTION

Jesus Prepares the Disciples

It was just prior to the Passover Festival, and Jesus was dining with the disciples in the Upper Room. Jesus knew that His time on earth was coming to a close. The announcement of His departure and pending arrival of the Holy Spirit follows several events that surprised and confused the disciples.

BIBLE LEARNING

AIM: Students will recognize that their reliance on and submission to the "Spirit of truth" will sometimes distinguish them from the world.

I. The Advocate is the Holy Spirit (John 14:15–17)

Jesus describes the relationship that exists between Himself and the disciples. The Greek verb translated as "keep" is *tereo* (Gk. **tay-REH-oh**), which has a sense of watching over or guarding. Tereo is in the future tense and can be translated "You will obey" (Mounce, 420). Obeying Jesus' commandments is a natural result of their love for Him. This is a statement of relationship, rather than a command. The disciples' love for Jesus will result in their adherence to His teachings.

Keeping the Commandments (verses 15–17)

15 If ye love me, keep my commandments.

Jesus begins this segment of the discourse with a conditional clause using the word "if" and ends with a a statement about the future ("keep my commandments"). The KJV and NLT translate this like a command, but it is a conditional with a simple future tense verb, not an imperative ("if you love me, you will keep"). The sense of the Greek is that the events of the conditional are not certain. As a result, Jesus is indicating that the disciples have a choice in the matter. They may choose to love Him, resulting in them keeping His commandments, or they may choose not to. It is not a lack of omniscience on Jesus' part that is of concern here but the free will of the disciples to love or not love Jesus. Jesus is saying that the proof of their love for Him is the keeping of His commandments. He would repeat this in various ways both in this chapter (**vv. 21, 23**) and in several other passages (e.g., **15:10**). John also reiterates this in his first epistle (**1 John 5:3**).

In **John 13:34**, Christ defines His "new" commandment as loving one another, and all that He has been teaching them is summed up in this one commandment of love. Keeping all of His commandments can be done by keeping this single one: love one another.

16 And I will pray the Father, and he shall give you another Comforter, that he may abide with you for ever;

The promise that follows seems to be directly linked with the preceding verse and the theme of loving obedience. It seems that His praying to the Father and the sending of the Comforter are conditional on the apostles' relationship with Him, evidenced by keeping His commandments. This relationship would motivate Him to pray (Gk. *erotao*, **eh-roh-TAH-oh**) to the Father on their behalf, and "he shall give you another Comforter."

Because of Jesus' prayer, "another Comforter" will come to the disciples. The word for "another" sheds light on the relationship of the Spirit to the Father and Son. It is not the word for "another of a different kind," *heteros* (Gk. **HEH-teh-ross**), but for "another of the same kind," which is *allos* (Gk. **AH-loss**). The word "Comforter" (Gk. *parakletos*, **pa-RAH-klaytose**) has the idea of one called alongside to help. Hence, the New American Standard Bible translates it as "Helper." It has the idea of one who stands by another and exhorts or encourages. It is also translated "Advocate" (NIV), meaning one called particularly in a law court to plead one's case (**1 John 2:1**), not as a professional pleader but as a friend.

This is the first of five times the function and activities of the Holy Spirit are mentioned in the discourse (see **14:25–26, 15:26–27, 16:5–15**). The idea here is that since Jesus is about to leave them, the Father will send the Holy Spirit, who will "abide with them forever." The duration of the presence of the Comforter on earth with the disciples and believers is not temporary as Jesus' presence was, but permanent—forever. He assures them that it is to their advantage that He depart so that the Holy Spirit would come and be with them permanently (**16:7**).

17 Even the Spirit of truth; whom the world cannot receive, because it seeth him not, neither knoweth him: but ye know him; for he dwelleth with you, and shall be in you.

This Comforter is called "the Spirit of truth." This defines one of the functions of the Holy Spirit. The word "Spirit" used here (Gk. *pneuma*, **puh-NEHOO-mah**, literally "wind" or "breath") is the same word Jesus used to describe to Nicodemus the function of the Spirit in conversion (**John 3:8**).

Truth is one of the characteristics of the Holy Spirit. This is not surprising, since truth is a recurrent theme in the Gospel of John (**1:17**). Jesus says earlier in this chapter that He is "the way, the truth, and the life" (**14:6**; cf. **8:32**). From these and other passages, we learn that Christ is the embodiment of truth. Here the Spirit shares the same nature with Christ and communicates truth (**15:26; 16:13**), testifying about Christ.

Jesus says the "world" (Gk. *kosmos*, **KOZ-mose**), here meaning the "unsaved," cannot receive this Spirit and gives two reasons for it. Firstly, they do not see Him because they are spiritually blind (see **2 Corinthians 4:4**). Secondly, they do not know Him because they refuse to believe or understand Him (see **1 Corinthians 2:14**).

Christ says the sinful nature of the world causes people to prefer darkness rather than light (**John 3:19**), and calls this kind of people children of the devil, for they desire to do their father's will (**John 8:44**). Only those who believe in the Gospel of Christ are able to receive and know the Spirit of truth (**1 John 4:6**). In contrast to the world, the disciples know the Spirit or have experienced Him because He dwells in them, Jesus says. They have this privilege of knowing Him because of their belief and relationship with Christ.

The next point of interest in this verse is the use of the present and the future tenses, "for he dwelleth with you, and shall be in you." Some interpret this as a continuation of the presence or indwelling of the Holy Spirit in the believer. This agrees with the previous verse: "that He may abide with you forever." Another interpretation is that while the Spirit dwells with them in a measure now, they would receive the Spirit in greater measure when He comes into their lives in

His fullness at the baptism of the Holy Spirit (see **John 3:34**; cf. **Matthew 3:11; Luke 11:13; John 1:31–33**). It is believed that this was fulfilled on the day of Pentecost in Acts.

QUESTION 1

What future event is Jesus referring to when He says that the Spirit will be in them (**John 14:17**)?

II. THE DISCIPLES ARE NOT ABANDONED (vv. 18–25)

Jesus doesn't intend to leave them fatherless. He will reveal Himself to the disciples after His death, burial, and resurrection. Not only will He visit them physically, but He will send His Spirit. His resurrection ensures that they will have new life (**vv. 19–20**). Modern-day believers also have this new life in Christ because of His sacrificial death and resurrection.

Jesus Reassures the Disciples (verses 18–25)

18 I will not leave you comfortless: I will come to you.

Jesus then assures His disciples of His continued presence. The word "comfortless" is the Greek *orphanos* (**or-fan-OSE**), from which we derive its English equivalent, "orphan." Other renderings of this word include "desolate" or "helpless." The next use of the word is found in **James 1:27**, where KJV renders it "fatherless."

Jesus promises to them further, saying, "I will come to you." Is He referring to His immediate appearance after His resurrection, which happens approximately three days after this speech (**John 20; Acts 1:3**)? Or, is He talking about His coming in the Person of the Holy Spirit, therefore carrying forward the same trend of thought of **verses 16 and 17**? Alternatively, is He talking about His Second Coming, a thought He started

with in this chapter (**vv. 1–3**)? All three are possible, and all three might be included in His thought.

19 Yet a little while, and the world seeth me no more; but ye see me: because I live, ye shall live also.

Jesus states that the world would not see Him because He would soon die and ascend into Heaven. He further clarifies that the disciples will be able to see Him, because He would live again and give them access to eternal life through the power of the Holy Spirit.

20 At that day ye shall know that I am in my Father, and ye in me, and I in you.

Here Jesus describes the nature of the relationship. He would have with the disciples and all who would subsequently follow Him. He says that they would know experientially that He was in the nature, soul, and thought of the Father; they would be in Him and He would be in them in the same manner. Although He would be away, the Spirit or Comforter would be in them and this would be their relational connection to Him.

21 He that hath my commandments, and keepeth them, he it is that loveth me: and he that loveth me shall be loved of my Father, and I will love him, and will manifest myself to him.

Jesus says that if the disciples not only have His commandments but obey them, it is proof that they love Him. This love for Him will be rewarded with love from both the Father and Son. Jesus says that He will manifest (Gk. *emphanizo*, **em-fa-NEED-zoh**) Himself to those who love Him. The word "manifest" means "to exhibit for view, to show one's self." This would happen through the coming of the Comforter, the Holy Spirit.

22 Judas saith unto him, not Iscariot, Lord, how is it that thou wilt manifest thyself unto us, and not unto the world?

This Judas shares his name with the disciple who betrayed Jesus. He asks how Jesus can show Himself to the disciples and not to the world. Jesus gives His answer in the next verse.

23 Jesus answered and said unto him, If a man love me, he will keep my words: and my Father will love him, and we will come unto him, and make our abode with him.

Jesus says that if a person loves Him and obeys His words, then the Father will love them, and Jesus and the Father will come to and make their abode with that person. Here Jesus is speaking of the indwelling of the Holy Spirit in the life of the believer. This will be the method in which Jesus will manifest Himself to His disciples.

24 He that loveth me not keepeth not my sayings: and the word which ye hear is not mine, but the Father's which sent me. 25 These things have I spoken unto you, being yet present with you.

Jesus goes back to the love motif again. Stating it negatively (cf. **v. 15**), He reinforces the truth about loving Him and keeping His "sayings" (Gk. *logos*, **LAH-goss**) or teachings. He says anyone who does not love Him would not keep His teachings. This is akin to **verse 17**, where we learned that the world cannot receive the Holy Spirit because they do not know Him.

In essence, he who rejects Christ will not even listen to His teachings, and in effect also rejects the Father since Jesus' teachings are the Father's (**Luke 10:16; John 3:36; 13:20**). Jesus refuses to take glory for Himself and says, "for all that I have heard of my Father

I have made known to you" (from **John 15:15**). Again He gives the Father total credit for His teachings.

QUESTION 2

How do you think the disciples might have felt as they heard Jesus talk about leaving them (**vv. 19, 25**)?

III. THE HOLY SPIRIT IS JESUS' REPRESENTATIVE (v. 26)

The Father will send the Holy Spirit to represent Christ in the world in the same way that Christ was sent to the world to represent God. In Jesus' absence, the Holy Spirit will remind the disciples of His teachings.

The Comforter Will Come (verse 26)

26 But the comforter, which is the Holy Ghost, whom the Father will send in my name, he shall teach you all things, and bring all things to your remembrance, whatsoever I have said unto you.

The conjunction "but" at the beginning of this verse clarifies the point of the previous verse. There Jesus seems to say, "Although I have been teaching you in person and will soon leave you, you are not losing anything, since you are about to receive the Comforter, the Holy Spirit, whose work includes bringing to your remembrance all My teachings." Here Christ mentions both the office and name of the Holy Spirit, both of which we have come across in the earlier verses of the chapter (**vv. 16–18**).

In **verse 17**, Jesus referred to the Third Person of the Trinity as the Spirit of Truth, but here He calls Him the Holy Spirit, intentionally distinguishing Him from any other spirit. As we have already noted in **verse 16**, the Holy Spirit is from the Father. The new thing here is that Jesus is the medium through whom the Holy Spirit will be sent. This is the significance of the Father sending the Spirit "in [Jesus'] name." The function of the Holy Spirit is to comfort, encourage, and communicate the truth. He also teaches (**v. 26**). He will both teach and remind us of Jesus' teachings. The work of the Holy Spirit is referenced here again in order to give the disciples confidence and encouragement to face Jesus' imminent departure. The Holy Spirit would have a dual function. He would both aid the disciples by recalling all that Jesus had taught them, and would also teach them Himself—even about future events (cf. **16:13**).

BIBLE APPLICATION

AIM: Students will rely on the power of the Holy Spirit to enable them to do what they otherwise could not do.

Life is more enjoyable when we walk alongside others who are willing to encourage and support one another. Have you ever encountered a problem that seemed impossible to solve until you asked for help from someone? Remember how relieved you felt when you didn't have to figure it out on your own? This is similar to the Holy Spirit's ministry in believers' lives. He has been given to come alongside us and instruct us in how to live. We are not alone.

STUDENTS' RESPONSES

AIM: Students will seek to express their love for Jesus through their obedience to His commands.

Ask God to reveal ways in which you can actively seek out the guidance of the Holy Spirit in your life. This might be as simple as praying for the guidance of the Holy Spirit in a situation.

Or, you might find yourself relying solely on your own understanding when making decisions. Instead, prayerfully consider what the Holy Spirit is leading you to do.

PRAYER

Sweet Holy Spirit, guide us in knowing what to do, and how to share God's love for us. Sweet Holy Spirit, we thank You for protecting us, and loving us. Allow us to actively seek Your faithful ways as we live and build God's Kingdom through Jesus. In Jesus' Name we pray. Amen.

DIG A LITTLE DEEPER

Perhaps there is no better way to internalize the significance of the Paraclete in our lives than to mimic Him by coming alongside others and providing support and advocacy. The Paraclete Mission Group serves and supports missions agencies, churches, and church-planting movements around the world. Paraclete enlists experienced missionaries and professionals so that these associates can more effectively use their life experiences, skills, and gifts to help individuals and ministry organizations.

One such associate, Sharon McElwain, was interviewed for the Paraclete blog site in October 2023. Ms. McElwain described her mission: "My current ministry is mostly quilting. I go to Garbage City in North Africa. People literally sit in the middle of garbage and sort it. That's their life. They live there, and they die there. I've been going there for over 15 years, once or twice a year, seeing the same people. We started out by being very careful with the Old Testament. And then, when the people trust me, I go to stories in the New Testament. They will sew for a while, and then we take a break. I tell a story and then ask them questions about it. And then we sew a while more. At the end, I ask them how I can pray for them. We have different conversations during that time. Because of the stories, they bring up questions. So, I share Jesus."

Paraclete supports many independent missionaries, like Ms. McElwain, but they also come alongside churches, para-church organizations, and kingdom-minded businesses and professionals. They prioritize Christian leaders who have limited resources, work among unreached people, or work in remote places. If you are interested in learning more about the ministry of Paraclete Mission Group, you can contact them through their website: https://www.paraclete.net/

Ref.: Manley, Jim. "Dumps and Guns—When I Hear His Voice I Obey." Associates, Paraclete.net, October 8, 2023.

HOW TO SAY IT

Motif.	mo-**TEEF**.
Iscariot.	Is-**KAIR**-ee-ut.

DAILY HOME BIBLE READINGS

MONDAY
Is There No Balm in Gilead?
(Jeremiah 8:18–22)

TUESDAY
No One to Comfort Me
(Lamentations 1:17–21)

WEDNESDAY
Here is Your God!
(Isaiah 40:1–10)

THURSDAY
This is My Comfort
(Psalm 119:49–64)

FRIDAY
The Shepherd's Comfort
(Psalm 23)

SATURDAY
When the Advocate Comes
(John 15:18–26)

SUNDAY
An Advocate with You Forever
(John 14:15–26)

PREPARE FOR NEXT SUNDAY

Read **John 16:4b–15** and study "The Spirit of Truth."

Sources:

Barker, Kenneth L. and John R. Kohlenberger III, eds. *The Expositor's Bible Commentary.* Abridged Edition, New Testament. Grand Rapids, MI: Zondervan, 1994. 346, 349.

Barker, Kenneth L. *Zondervan Study Bible.* TNIV. Grand Rapids, MI: Zondervan, 2006. 1807–1810.

Butler, Trent C., ed. "Fatherless." *Holman Bible Dictionary.* Electronic Edition, Quickverse. Nashville, TN: Holman Bible Publishers, 1991.

Butler, Trent C., ed. "Passover." *Holman Bible Dictionary.* Electronic Edition, Quickverse. Nashville, TN: Holman Bible Publishers, 1991.

Carson, D. A. *The Gospel According to John: Pillar New Testament Commentary.* Grand Rapids, MI: Wm. B. Eerdmans Publishing Company, 1991. 498–510.

Mounce, William D. and Mounce, Robert H., eds. *The Zondervan Greek and English Interlinear New Testament.* Grand Rapids, MI: Zondervan, 2008. 420.

Thayer, Joseph. "Entole." *Thayer's Greek Definitions.* 3rd ed. Electronic Edition, Quickverse. El Cajon, CA: Institute for Creation Research, 1999.

Thayer, Joseph. "Parakletos." *Thayer's Greek Definitions.* 3rd ed. Electronic Edition, Quickverse. El Cajon, CA: Institute for Creation Research, 1999.

Walvoord, John F. and Zuck, Roy B., eds. *The Bible Knowledge Commentary: An Exposition of the Scriptures.* Wheaton, IL: Victor Books, 1983. 323–324.

COMMENTS / NOTES:

_____
_____
_____
_____
_____
_____
_____
_____
_____
_____
_____
_____
_____
_____
_____
_____
_____
_____
_____
_____
_____

THE SPIRIT OF TRUTH

BIBLE BASIS: John 16:4b–15

BIBLE TRUTH: Jesus promised the disciples that the Holy Spirit would be a real presence to them and this promise is true for all believers.

MEMORY VERSE: "Nevertheless I tell you the truth; It is expedient for you that I go away: for if I go not away, the Comforter will not come unto you; but if I depart, I will send him unto you" (John 16:7).

LESSON AIM: By the end of the lesson, your students will: learn what Jesus says about how the Holy Spirit works on our behalf; express their feelings about the loss of those close to them; and find ways to tell others about how the Holy Spirit works on our behalf.

BIBLE BACKGROUND: John 16:4b–15; 1 Samuel 3:1–10--Read and incorporate the insights gained from the Background Scriptures into your study of the lesson.

LESSON SCRIPTURE

JOHN 16:4b–15, KJV

4 And these things I said not unto you at the beginning, because I was with you.

5 But now I go my way to him that sent me; and none of you asketh me, Whither goest thou?

6 But because I have said these things unto you, sorrow hath filled your heart.

7 Nevertheless I tell you the truth; It is expedient for you that I go away: for if I go not away, the Comforter will not come unto you; but if I depart, I will send him unto you.

8 And when he is come, he will reprove the world of sin, and of righteousness, and of judgment:

9 Of sin, because they believe not on me;

10 Of righteousness, because I go to my Father, and ye see me no more;

11 Of judgment, because the prince of this world is judged.

12 I have yet many things to say unto you, but ye cannot bear them now.

13 Howbeit when he, the Spirit of truth, is come, he will guide you into all truth: for he shall not speak of himself; but whatsoever he shall hear, that shall he speak: and he will shew you things to come.

14 He shall glorify me: for he shall receive of mine, and shall shew it unto you.

15 All things that the Father hath are mine: therefore said I, that he shall take of mine, and shall shew it unto you.

BIBLICAL DEFINITIONS

A. Comforter (John 16:7) *Parakletos(Gk.)—One* who encourages, helps, pleads the case for or represents another.

B. Reprove (v. 8) *elegcho* (Gk.)—To correct or criticize someone with the purpose of convincing him or her of sin or wrongdoing.

LIFE NEED FOR TODAY'S LESSON

AIM: Students will allow the Holy Spirit to guide us and trust Him to find people who can help us.

INTRODUCTION

Expect the Holy Spirit

This Gospel is attributed to John, son of Zebedee and one of Christ's closest disciples. His purpose for writing the book is found in **John 20:31**: "But these are written, that ye might believe that Jesus is the Christ, the Son of God; and that believing ye might have life through his name."

In this particular passage, Christ tells His disciples to expect the Holy Spirit, who will reveal more of the truth of who He is (His glory). The immediate recipients of His instructions were His apostles, but the principles also apply to His future followers.

BIBLE LEARNING

AIM: Students will trust that the Holy Spirit is helping them just as surely as if Jesus is present in the flesh to give them aid.

I. THE COMING OF THE HOLY SPIRIT (JOHN 16:4b–7)

Continuing His instructions, Jesus tells the disciples that after He leaves them, an Advocate will arrive—the Holy Spirit. While they were understandably sad, He pointed out that they were so consumed with how His leaving affected them in the present, they were missing the future benefit—the Holy Spirit, who will abide with them forever **(14:16)**. Jesus says that it would be expedient for Him to leave, because this would prepare the way for the Holy Spirit to come.

Persecution and Trouble Ahead (verses 4b–7)

4b And these things I said not unto you at the beginning, because I was with you.

Jesus had not needed to tell them about persecution and future troubles because He was present with them. From the very beginning, they had walked with Jesus and learned from Him. They had assisted Him in performing miracles and witnessed signs and wonders. They were His disciples. The Pharisees and the teachers of the law confronted Him and not His students. He was there to take the brunt of the attacks and be a shield to protect them. Soon He would leave, and they would be confronted as the ones who followed and learned from Him.

5 But now I go my way to him that sent me; and none of you asketh me, Whither goest thou?

In **John 14:5**, Thomas had asked, "Lord, we don't know where you are going, so how can we know the way?" (NIV). He doesn't ask Jesus where He is going but makes a statement about how confused he is by Jesus' pronouncement of going away. Jesus states that He is going "to him that sent me." This should have aroused curiosity within the disciples. If they followed Jesus for such a long time, they should have been hungry to know who sent Him. Jesus was speaking of His ascension to Heaven to return to the Father. The confusion of the disciples indicates that they must have only thought of Jesus' departure on a purely physical level.

6 But because I have said these things unto you, sorrow hath filled your heart.

The disciples were sad because Jesus was leaving them. They didn't understand that He was referring to His ascension and that He was going to the Father. They were merely thinking on an earthly level and did not realize that Jesus is the Son of God, sent to earth to die and rise again. At this point they were only thinking of Him as an earthly rabbi who taught them things and performed some miracles. As a result, when Jesus talks about leaving, sorrow fills their hearts. They don't understand the broader spiritual implications.

7 Nevertheless I tell you the truth; It is expedient for you that I go away: for if I go not away, the Comforter will not come unto you; but if I depart, I will send him unto you.

In this section, Jesus tells them how important and necessary it is that He should leave them. Unless He departs, the Spirit will not come. He has already told them about the persecution they will encounter and the sorrow they will have at His leaving. There is a definite advantage for the disciples that He departs, because then the Spirit (Counselor) would come. "Expedient" (Gk. *sumphero*, **soom-FAIR-oh**) means profitable, beneficial, or for one's good. This word is used two other times in John (**11:50; 18:14**), and in both of these passages, the verb refers to Jesus' death and the fact that it will benefit everyone. After Jesus ascends to Heaven, the Spirit would then be with the disciples and those who came after Him, no matter where they found themselves. It was also expedient because as Jesus explains in the next verse, the Comforter would come with a definite agenda of convicting the world. This was something that could not happen until the ascension of Christ into Heaven.

The use of the word "Comforter" adds another specific dimension in the activities of the Holy Spirit in view of the persecution that would come to them. The word in Greek is *parakletos* (**pah-RAH-klay-tose**), which can mean comforter, advocate or helper. In this passage, the Spirit takes on all of these roles in different ways as one who convicts the world and serves as God's messenger to believers and the world.

The phrase "I will send him unto you" and other passages indicate the manner in which the Holy Spirit is sent to us. He is the gift of God who emanates from the Father (**14:16, 26**) and is sent by the Son (**15:26, 16:7**; cf. **Luke 24:49**). Humans have no part in initiating the process. God takes the initiative. Furthermore, the coming of the Spirit, as we have noted, depends on the departure of Jesus (**16:7**; cf. **7:39**).

II. WORK OF THE HOLY SPIRIT: CONVICTION (vv. 8–11)

This Advocate would have a different role in believers' and unbelievers' lives. Ultimately He would function as a guide for both. The guidance of the Holy Spirit for unbelievers would be in the direction of initially submitting to the Lordship of Christ and turning away from sin. John refers to those who don't believe as "the world." This does not refer to the physical creation, but everyone who does not follow Jesus.

Judgment and the Holy Spirit (verses 8–11)

8 And when he is come, he will reprove the world of sin, and of righteousness, and of judgment: 9 Of sin, because they believe not on me; 10 Of righteousness, because I go to the Father, and ye see me no more; 11 Of judgment, because the prince of this world is judged.

These four verses constitute some of the fundamental beliefs in the Christian doctrine concerning the work of the Holy Spirit in the process of conversion. In them, Jesus reveals what hitherto has not been stressed, i.e., the Spirit's work to reprove or convict. The word "reprove" (Gk. *elegkho*, **el-ENG-kho**) means to convict, convince, or expose.

Jesus describes the threefold work of conviction by the Holy Spirit. Firstly, He will convict the world of sin. The Holy Spirit will cause people to recognize their sinfulness in the sight of God. This includes the major sin of not believing in Christ. This rejection of the Gospel of Christ (and the rejection of His person) is the most serious offense because without Christ, all the other sins committed by a person cannot be forgiven.

Secondly, the Spirit convicts the world of righteousness. Here He will bring to their consciousness the standard of righteousness that God demands from all. That standard of righteousness is Christ, and without His presence in the world, we are at a loss for the true standard of what God requires for humanity. The "righteousness" here that God requires is communicated by the Greek word *dikaiosune* (**dee-keye-oh-SOO-nay**), which can also be translated "justification." It means being judicially right in the sight of God. Human justification is the gift of God through our belief in Christ. It is not earned; it is the work of faith.

The third work of the Spirit is to convict the world of judgment, "because the prince of this world is judged." The prince or ruler of this world refers to Satan (see **John 12:31, 14:30; 2 Corinthians 4:4; Ephesians 2:2; 1 John 4:4**). Satan is the author and source of all evil and unbelief. The word "judged" (Gk. *krino*, **KREE-no**) is the language of a court of law and has the idea of being condemned. The noun form speaks of decision, passing a judgment, or verdict by a jury or a tribunal. The world, of course, is the world system ruled by Satan and the devil, whom Jesus referred to as their father (see **John 8:44**). Therefore, Jesus says that those who refuse to believe in the Gospel face the same fate of condemnation as their master, the devil has already received (see **Luke 10:18–20; John 3:36; Revelation 20:11–15, 21:8**). The actual condemnation or defeat of the prince of this world will be accomplished on the Cross. We see the work of the Holy Spirit is to reveal or expose not only the sin of unbelief, but also its result of judgment or condemnation, which awaits unbelievers. The Holy Spirit, on the one hand, brings people to the consciousness of their sins and leads them to repent and believe in the Gospel, while on the other hand, He also condemns those who refuse to repent, just like their master the devil.

QUESTION 1

What is the Holy Spirit's role to the world (**John 16:8–11**)?

III. WORK OF THE HOLY SPIRIT: GUIDANCE (vv. 12–15)

The Holy Spirit would come not only to convict the world, but guide believers as the Spirit of truth. The apostles were used to having Christ as their rabbi, teaching and guiding them. Now, they would have to rely on the Holy Spirit. Jesus comments that He has more to tell them but they could not bear it. When the Holy Spirit comes then He would lead them and guide them into all the truth that they could not handle at that moment.

Teachings from the Holy Spirit (verses 12–15)

12 I have yet many things to say unto you, but ye cannot bear them now.

The above sayings are no doubt hard to understand even to the disciples. They are perplexed and cannot make sense of what He is saying. Jesus recognizes their plight and says that He understands their situation. He realizes that they cannot comprehend all that He has been teaching—either the teachings are so highly spiritual that the disciples cannot fully understand them, or the disciples are so filled with emotion that they find it hard to bear the news of His imminent departure. Therefore, Jesus tells them that although He still has lots of things to tell them, He will not do so. The reason is they "cannot bear them now." "Bear" (Gk. *bastazo*, **bahs-TAD-zoh**) translates to carry, or bear something heavy or burdensome. In view of their emotional state, they could not carry the weight of what He wanted to say to them. It would be too much for them to take it all in. What are the things that would be too hard for them? They include "things to come" (**v. 13**), both to the immediate future and the end time events.

13 Howbeit when he, the Spirit of truth, is come, he will guide you into all truth: for he shall not speak of himself; but whatsoever he shall hear, that shall he speak: and he will shew you things to come.
14 He shall glorify me: for he shall receive of mine, and shall shew it unto you.
15 All things that the Father hath are mine: therefore said I, that he shall take of mine, and shall shew it unto you.

In this section, Jesus continues to explain to them the work of the Holy Spirit, whom He names the Spirit of Truth (**14:17, 26**; cf. **1 John 4:6**). His mission here is to guide the believer into all truth about Christ, not of Himself. He will be the medium of God's communication to mankind. Through the communication of the Holy Spirit, Christ will be glorified (cf. **vv. 8–11; 15:26**), because the Holy Spirit will not speak on His own authority, but whatever Christ reveals to Him (cf. **14:24**). The word "glorified" (*doxadzo*, **dok-SAHD-zo**) means to cause the dignity and worth of some person or thing to become manifest and acknowledged. Whatever can be known about Jesus, the Spirit will reveal to the disciples. Because Jesus is

God incarnate, the Spirit will glorify Him by communicating for Him and about Him to believers. What would the Spirit receive from Jesus? The truth about Jesus. He would communicate the truth about Jesus to the disciples and to the world. This would lead to Jesus being glorified.

In **verse 15**, Jesus equates Himself with the Father since the revelation is from both the Father and the Son through the Spirit. Here we see that God's Word—all truth—is a combined work of the Trinity.

QUESTION 2

What is one of the Holy Spirit's roles to the apostles and believers (**vv. 12–15**)?

BIBLE APPLICATION

AIM: Students will trust that the Holy Spirit is helping them just as surely as if Jesus is present in the flesh to give them aid.

We live during a time when people mistakenly believe they can create their own truths depending upon how they feel, what they believe, and how much energy they put toward it. However, not believing something is true does not make it false. If a person does not believe the sky is blue, it does not change the reality that it is. The Holy Spirit is as living and active now as He was in John's day. He still points people to truth, using God's Word and other people. The Spirit of truth still convicts of sin, righteousness, and judgment. He still guides into all truth—just not those truths that make people comfortable.

STUDENTS' RESPONSES

AIM: Students will tell others about the presence and transforming power the Holy Spirit in their lives.

The Holy Spirit still reveals sinners' need for Christ and works to convince them to believe in Him. If there are people in your life who do not believe in Christ, pray for them. Ask God for opportunities, grace, and wisdom through the Holy Spirit to share His truth with them.

PRAYER

Dear Jesus, the Comforter is a reminder of Your love and sacrifice for us and the world. As we allow the Holy Spirit to teach us and show us the way, let us ever be mindful of how we are to care for one another. In Jesus' Name we pray. Amen.

DIG A LITTLE DEEPER

How do we fulfill the challenge posed by our lesson aim, to "find ways to tell others about how the Holy Spirit works on our behalf"? There is an interesting metaphor of "spiritual breathing" that may help us explain the work of the Spirit. A comparison is made with natural breathing, which is necessary to sustain our physical lives. "Spiritual breathing, like physical breathing," said Bill Bright, founder of Campus Crusade for Christ, "is a process of exhaling the impure and inhaling the pure, an exercise in faith that enables you to experience God's love and forgiveness and walk in the Spirit as a way of life." In the metaphor, we "exhale" by expelling our sins through confession to God and trust in His forgiveness. We "inhale" by drawing in the power of the Holy Spirit and yielding to His control. Unlike physical breathing, which is automatic, spiritual breathing requires our active participation. Breathing out is how we accept the Spirit's reproof of sin, righteousness and judgment. Breathing in is how we receive the fullness of the Spirit in our lives (the fruit, the gifts, and the witnessing power). It is a conscious choice to experience all that Jesus promised us.

Ref.: Wiebe, Stacy. "Spiritual Oxygen: Are You Getting It?" The Life (blog). https://thelife.com/spiritual-oxygen-are-you-getting-it

HOW TO SAY IT

Expedient. eks-**PEE**-dee-ent.

Reprove. ri-**PROOV**.

Zebedee. **ZEH**-buh-dee.

DAILY HOME BIBLE READINGS

MONDAY
Where There is No Prophecy
(Proverbs 29:12–18)

TUESDAY
The Lord Has Closed Your Eyes
(Isaiah 29:8–14)

WEDNESDAY
Speak, for Your Servant is
Listening (1 Samuel 3:1–10)

THURSDAY
A Trustworthy Prophet of the
Lord (1 Samuel 3:11–21)

FRIDAY
I Commit My Spirit
(Psalm 31:1–8)

SATURDAY
Worship in Spirit and Truth
(John 4:21–26)

SUNDAY
The Spirit of Truth Will Guide
You (John 16:4b–15)

PREPARE FOR NEXT SUNDAY

Read **John 20:19–23** and study "Receive the Holy Spirit."

Sources:
Grudem, Wayne. *Bible Doctrine.* Grand Rapids, MI: Zondervan, 1999. 104-110. *Hebrew-Greek Key Word Study Bible.* King James Version. Chattanooga, TN: AMG Publishers, Inc., 1991.
Keener, Craig S. *The IVP Bible Background Commentary: New Testament.* Downers Grove, IL: Intervarsity Press, 1993. 260–263, 302–303.

Radmacher, Earl D., ed. *Nelson Study Bible*. New King James Version. Nashville, TN: Thomas Nelson Publishers, 1997. 1754–1755, 1792–1800.

Ryrie, Charles C. *Ryrie Study Bible*. New International Version. Chicago, IL: Moody Press. 1986. 1480–1481.

Unger, Merrill F. *The New Unger's Bible Dictionary*. Chicago, IL: Moody Press, 1988. 410–411.

Walvoord, John F., and Roy B. Zuck, eds. *The Bible Knowledge Commentary: New Testament*. Wheaton, IL: Victor Books, SP Publications, Inc., 1983. 327–329.

Zondervan Study Bible. *New International Version*. Grand Rapids, MI: Zondervan Publishers, 2002. 1661–1662.

COMMENTS / NOTES:

RECEIVE THE HOLY SPIRIT

BIBLE BASIS: John 20:19–23

BIBLE TRUTH: Jesus speaks peace to and empowers all His disciples with the gift of the Holy Spirit.

MEMORY VERSE: "And when he had said this, he breathed on them, and saith unto them, Receive ye the Holy Ghost" (John 20:22).

LESSON AIM: By the end of the lesson, your students will: explore the importance of Jesus' appearance to the disciples; describe their feelings from times when the words of others calmed their fears; and perform the mission God has for their lives as empowered by the Holy Spirit.

BIBLE BACKGROUND: John 20:19–23; Acts 1:4–8, 2:1–4; Romans 14:13–19—Read and incorporate the insights gained from the Background Scriptures into your study of the lesson.

LESSON SCRIPTURE

JOHN 20:19–23, KJV

19 Then the same day at evening, being the first day of the week, when the doors were shut where the disciples were assembled for fear of the Jews, came Jesus and stood in the midst, and saith unto them, Peace be unto you.

20 And when he had so said, he shewed unto them his hands and his side. Then were the disciples glad, when they saw the LORD.

21 Then said Jesus to them again, Peace be unto you: as my Father hath sent me, even so send I you.

22 And when he had said this, he breathed on them, and saith unto them, Receive ye the Holy Ghost:

23 Whose soever sins ye remit, they are remitted unto them; and whose soever sins ye retain, they are retained.

BIBLICAL DEFINITIONS

A. Remit (John 20:23) *aphiemi* (Gk.)—To dismiss, forsake, leave, to forgive debts or sins.

B. Retain (v. 23) *krateo* (Gk.)—To hold onto, not remit, or seize control of.

LIFE NEED FOR TODAY'S LESSON

AIM: Students will will know that there is power in the tongue and that Jesus speaks power into our lives.

INTRODUCTION

Jesus Visits the Disciples

After spending several years with the man claiming to be the Messiah and Son of God, and seeing Him perform untold numbers of miracles (so many that "if they should be written every one … the world itself could not contain the books that should be written," **John 21:25**), it was disheartening for the disciples to witness His death. The disciples knew Christ's miraculous power. They had seen Him escape from His enemies several times. They, like many Jews, were expecting Him to be a triumphant King who would free them from their oppressors, the Romans, and usher in a new worldly kingdom (**Luke 24:21, John 6:15**). But He was dead. Not only that, but because of the hostility of the Jewish leaders, they feared for their lives, locking themselves behind closed doors. Christ promises that they would go on to "greater works" (**John 14:12**) looked grim.

BIBLE LEARNING

AIM: Students will receive and claim the power of the Holy Spirit in their work for the Lord.

1. CHRIST APPEARS TO THE DISCIPLES (John 20:19–20)

After appearing to Mary Magdalene at the tomb very early Sunday morning, Christ paid a visit to the majority of His disciples, although Thomas was not there (**v. 24**). This would be one of many visits that Christ would give to His disciples before ascending to heaven. What makes this visit special is the words that Christ speaks to them that foretell their upcoming mission. As they gathered in fear, Jesus arrives—despite locked doors—and brings a greeting of peace. While "peace be with you" was a common Jewish greeting in those days, Christ's words carry several meanings.

Jesus Visits the Disciples (verses 19–20)

19 Then the same day at evening, being the first day of the week, when the doors were shut where the disciples were assembled for fear of the Jews, came Jesus and stood in the midst, and saith unto them, Peace be unto you.

In these verses, the resurrected Jesus appears to a group of His followers for the first time. In the previous verses, the Resurrection was only witnessed by individuals. First, Jesus appears to Mary alone as she visits the tomb. Then Peter and the other disciple (assumed to be John) arrive at the empty tomb. Although they do not see Jesus, the empty tomb and His grave clothes neatly wrapped

and laid to the side are enough to cause them to believe. This occurs on Sunday, suggesting the practice of Christians gathering on that day, the first day of the week, corresponding with **verse 1**. Ten of the 11 disciples were gathered together after the crisis of seeing their rabbi, Jesus, arrested and executed by the Jewish rulers and Roman government. As a result, the disciples were fearful of the Jewish leaders and hid themselves from public sight. They did not want to risk being seen in public since their previous association with Jesus was widely known.

The doors were shut. Having the doors locked was a measure of precaution, but here it is mentioned with a reference to the appearance of Jesus. Locked doors proved to not be a barrier to His resurrected body. This suggests that the normal limitations of our bodies will be removed in the resurrection. It also suggests that nothing can keep Jesus from engaging our human condition. Our fears and anxieties cannot keep Jesus from coming to stand with us in whatever situation we find ourselves in. "Peace be with you" was a common Jewish greeting (Shalom), meaning "May all be well with you." As a Jew speaking to Jews, this word had additional connotations of prosperity, health, and blessing. Although this word was common in Jewish culture, when spoken by the Messiah, it means infinitely more. When Jesus says "peace," He actively gives what the word means. Peace is here presented as a gift from the risen Christ.

20 And when he had so said, he showed unto them his hands and his side. Then were the disciples glad, when they saw the LORD.

The risen Christ now reveals the genuineness of this gift before the eyes of the disciples. Jesus shows them the price with which He bought their peace: His pierced hands, His spear-pierced side, evidence of His death by crucifixion. These holy wounds proclaim that Jesus is at peace with the believers. The word *deiknumi* (Gk., **DAYK-noo-me**), to show, is a word that also means to give evidence or proof of thing. Showing His hands and His side would be unmistakable evidence that the same Jesus walked with them and who was crucified was now appearing among them. The disciples were glad because they saw the Lord. Doubt did not disappear all at once. Jesus appeared again and again, intensifying faith and joy, until nothing could ever disturb the solid certainty of their belief.

II. CHRIST COMMISSIONS THE DISCIPLES (vv. 21–23)

In the Bible, phrases that are repeated are often important. In this short passage, Christ exhorts His disciples to be at peace twice. He has proven that He has risen. He now encourages them: "Peace to you!" They no longer need to fear their persecutors, because God is with them. And, despite abandoning Him, they are not disqualified from service. He assures them that just as God sent Him to earth to fulfill a mission, He is sending them into the world to do the same. But He not only sends them, He equips them.

Greetings in Peace (verses 21–23)

21 Then said Jesus to them again, Peace be unto you: as my Father hath sent me, even so send I you.

"Peace be unto you" is a repetition of the first greeting. Jesus repeats this phrase for a number of possible reasons. One possibility is that the first time was intended to take away fear, while the second time was to call attention to the seriousness of His commission. Another possibility is that Jesus wanted to encourage them in the mission that He was sending them to do. He wanted them to know that although they would experience trials and difficulties, His peace would be with them. Jesus then commissions the disciples using relational analogies: "As the Father has sent me, so I send you." By this commission, the believers now bear the same divine authorization as Christ. Jesus has been sent into the world for a specific task and purpose, mainly His death and resurrection. The disciples are now authorized for the specific purpose of witnessing to His death and resurrection. They are authorized and commissioned to the task of dispensing this gift of peace in a troubled world. Jesus' Gospel is the Gospel of peace. Jesus Himself is our peace. He gives it to the disciples because those who bring peace must have peace.

Here the word *apostello* (Gk. **ah-po-STELL-oh**) is used for the Father sending Jesus. Jesus uses another word for His sending of the disciples into the world: *pempo* (Gk. **PEHM-po**). This word means to send or thrust, but does not carry authoritative connotation. The emphasis is on the specific action of sending or thrusting out. Jesus is saying just as the Father authorized and commissioned Him for a specific task, He would send or thrust His disciples out into the world.

22 And when he had said this, he breathed on them, and saith unto them, Receive ye the Holy Ghost.

He who sends enables those whom He sends, by the empowerment of the Holy Spirit. "Breathed on them" (Gk. *emphusao*, **em-foo-SAH-oh**) recalls the ancient association of spirit with breath and invokes **Genesis 2:7**. Jesus breathes on them in the same way that God breathed on Adam after shaping and forming him from the dust. This signifies that the church would be a new humanity created in the image of Christ. By breathing on them, Jesus foreshadows what would happen some weeks later on the day of Pentecost as the Spirit filled the house where they were praying like a mighty rushing wind. They would be empowered by the Holy Spirit for the commission that He has just given them. Jesus was filled with the Spirit at the start of His ministry; it would be no less so for the disciples.

The word for receive (Gk. *lambano*, **lam-BAHno**) is in the imperative mood, which indicates a command. Jesus is not inviting them to receive the Holy Spirit. It is not an option. He is commanding them to receive the Holy Spirit. By using this form of the verb, Jesus implies that the Holy Spirit is indispensable, necessary for the task that He has given them.

23 Whose soever sins ye remit, they are remitted unto them; and whose soever sins ye retain, they are retained.

With this act comes the responsibility to execute the divine will among believers and all humanity in the form of forgiveness. By this act, the risen Christ transforms fear into a great joy. The gift of the Spirit is to empower the disciples to exercise the right and authority with which He now clothes them in their sending. Jesus wants the remission of sins dispensed to sinners through the believers as His church on earth, excluding only those who refuse remission.

Two words are signi ficant: "remit" and "retain." To remit (Gk. *aphiemi*, **ah-FEE-ey-mee**) means to send away. Here the sins are removed from the sinner, as far as the east is from the west (see **Psalm 103:12**), blotting out the transgressions so that the Lord Himself will not remember them (see **Isaiah 43:25**). Forgiveness is infinite. To retain (Gk. *krateo*, **krah-TEH-oh**) is to hold fast with strength. The sins commit-

ted are not able to be let go. The moment a sin is committed, that sin with all its guilt adheres to the sinner, and no human effort can possibly blot it out. Only one person is able to remove that sin, to remove it as though it had never existed: Jesus Christ our Lord. It is still Jesus who dismisses or holds sins, yet by this act that empowers the disciples, He makes them His agents. He acts through them.

QUESTIONS 1 & 2

What phrase does Christ use twice (**John 20:19, 21**)?

What is the disciples' mission (**vv. 22, 23**)?

BIBLE APPLICATION

AIM: Students will be convinced that the risen Christ appeared to the disciples and serve Him with the conviction that He is alive.

We have the tendency to underestimate the power of one and the power of the tongue. Genocide has occurred because one person determined that certain people were not worthy of living and convinced others to go along with his views. In other instances, one man or woman with a vision has sparked movements, inspired change, and positively altered the course of history. Just one.

STUDENTS' RESPONSES

AIM: Students will speak words of reassurance to those whose faith is weak or faltering.

There is work to be done for God's glory. What passion has God given you? What problems do you see that you sense God has wired you to be part of solving? What stops you? Write this out, and place it somewhere you will see it often. Pray that God would equip you with His Spirit to fulfill the mission He has given you.

PRAYER

Dear Lord, let us live out the varied experiences that You have for us that molds and shapes our many purposes in life and honors You. Through the many skills, talents, and gifts that You have provided for us, let us give glory to Your name. In Jesus' Name we pray. Amen.

DIG A LITTLE DEEPER

When the worldwide Church celebrated the 500th anniversary of the Protestant Reformation (in recognition of how Martin Luther posted his 95 Theses on the door of the Wittenberg Castle Church), many commentators began to look back on Luther's life and ministry to assess the influence of that giant of the faith. Steve Strang, the founder of Charisma magazine, had an interesting Pentecostal perspective on Luther. In his research, he observed how the German theologian described his relationship with the Holy Spirit.

"But who enlightens our blind hearts?" Luther asked rhetorically in his Small Catechism. "The Holy Ghost, who is the true love and flame in God, alone can do that. He is poured out into our hearts, makes us be born again, and kindles a new light in us, and brings us to the knowledge of God the Father and His Son…" In one sermon, Luther wrote "You see very clearly that the Holy Spirit's office is not to write books nor to make laws, but freely to abrogate them… and that he is a God who writes only in the heart, who makes it burn, and create new courage. So that man grows happy before God, filled with love toward him, and with a happy heart serves the people." Luther didn't speak of the Spirit merely empowering his ministry, but he considered the Holy Ghost to be the animating influence on all aspects of his saved life.

Strang found that he had to reevaluate the assumption that the Church had forgotten the doctrine of the Holy Ghost from when the last apostle died until Pentecostalism was born in the early 20th Century. During the Middle Ages in Europe, voices like Luther's were actually asserting that the Spirit is intimately involved in the believer's life. Strang remarked that the anniversary of the Protestant Reformation reminded us that "the Holy Spirit has moved all through history, and that many movements had not only manifestations we now consider charismatic but also the kind of fervency and devotion to God we long for today." The mainline churches may not understand it, but the Church Universal has always celebrated the work of the Holy Ghost.

Ref.: Strang, Steve. "Martin Luther Understood the Work of the Holy Spirit." Perspective (column), Charisma, October 2017, p. 66.

HOW TO SAY IT

Pentecost.   **PEN**-teh-cost.

Shalom.   sha-**LOME**.

DAILY HOME BIBLE READINGS

MONDAY
The Holy Spirit Speaks
(Mark 13:5–11)

TUESDAY
Gentiles Receive the Holy Spirit
(Acts 10:39–48)

WEDNESDAY
Full of the Spirit and Faith
(Acts 11:19–26)

THURSDAY
Joy in the Holy Spirit
(Romans 14:13–19)

FRIDAY
Power from the Holy Spirit
(Acts 1:4–8)

SATURDAY
Be Filled with the Spirit
(Ephesians 5:15–21)

SUNDAY
Receive the Holy Spirit
(John 20:19–23)

PREPARE FOR NEXT SUNDAY
Read **Mark 11:1–11** and study "Love One Another."

Sources:
Hebrew-Greek Key Word Study Bible. King James Version.
Chattanooga, TN: AMG Publishers, Inc., 1991.
Keener, Craig S. *The IVP Bible Background Commentary: New Testament.* Downers Grove, IL: Intervarsity Press, 1993. 315–317.
Radmacher, Earl D., ed. *Nelson Study Bible.* New King James Version. Nashville, TN: Thomas Nelson Publishers, 1997. 1807–1808.
Ryrie, Charles C. *Ryrie Study Bible.* New International Version. Chicago, IL: Moody Press. 1986. 1487-1489.
Unger, Merrill F. *The New Unger's Bible Dictionary.* Chicago, IL: Moody Press, 1988. 1074–1075.
Walvoord, John F., and Roy B. Zuck, eds. *The Bible Knowledge Commentary: New Testament.* Wheaton, IL: Victor Books, SP Publications, Inc., 1983. 341–343.
Zondervan Study Bible. New International Version. Grand Rapids, MI: Zondervan Publishers, 2002. 1669–1670.

COMMENTS / NOTES:

LOVE ONE ANOTHER

BIBLE BASIS: 1 John 3:11–24

BIBLE TRUTH: John's letter indicates that the measure of people's lives is calculated by their faith in Christ and their love for one another.

MEMORY VERSE: "For this is the message that ye heard from the beginning, that we should love one another" (1 John 3:11).

LESSON AIM: By the end of the lesson, your students will: understand John's message about loving one another; affirm the fundamental discipleship principle of love for God and others; and express unconditional love to others.

BIBLE BACKGROUND: Mark 11:1–11; Isaiah 45:20–25—Read and incorporate the insights gained from the Background Scriptures into your study of the lesson.

LESSON SCRIPTURE

1 John 3:11–24, KJV

11 For this is the message that ye heard from the beginning, that we should love one another.

12 Not as Cain, who was of that wicked one, and slew his brother. And wherefore slew he him? Because his own works were evil, and his brother's righteous.

13 Marvel not, my brethren, if the world hate you.

14 We know that we have passed from death unto life, because we love the brethren. He that loveth not his brother abideth in death.

15 Whosoever hateth his brother is a murderer: and ye know that no murderer hath eternal life abiding in him.

16 Hereby perceive we the love of God, because he laid down his life for us: and we ought to lay down our lives for the brethren.

17 But whoso hath this world's good, and seeth his brother have need, and shutteth up his bowels of compassion from him, how dwelleth the love of God in him?

18 My little children, let us not love in word, neither in tongue; but in deed and in truth.

19 And hereby we know that we are of the truth, and shall assure our hearts before him.

20 For if our heart condemn us, God is greater than our heart, and knoweth all things.

21 Beloved, if our heart condemn us not, then have we confidence toward God.

22 And whatsoever we ask, we receive of him, because we keep his commandments, and do those things that are pleasing in his sight.

23 And this is his commandment, That we should believe on the name of his Son Jesus Christ, and love one another, as he gave us commandment.

24 And he that keepeth his commandments dwelleth in him, and he in him. And hereby we know that he abideth in us, by the Spirit which he hath given us.

BIBLICAL DEFINITIONS

A. Hosanna (Mark 11:9–10) *hosanna(Gk.)—From* the Hebrew words yasha' (ya-SHAW, to save) and na' (NAH, now).

B. Blessed (vv. 9–10) *eulogeo* (Gk.)— To praise, celebrate with praises.

LIFE NEED FOR TODAY'S LESSON

AIM: Students will experience the hatred of the world and counter it with God's love.

INTRODUCTION

Our Actions Reflect Our Love

This letter is written to members of the churches in Asia Minor. The epistle serves as a reminder to the children of God to love one another. The devil is the originator of sin and has sinned from the beginning of time. Those who belong to Satan reveal their essential nature by living lawless lives. This lawlessness is clearly seen in the blatant disregard for human life. John restates that Jesus laid the foundation on how we should treat one another. When Jesus died on the Cross, He demonstrated the greatest, truest, and most unselfish kind of love. His death validated that love is more than mere words; it must be followed by actions. When we say we love someone, our actions should prove our declaration. Displaying love for one another is evidence that we belong to God. Children of God should live to please the Lord in accordance with His commandments. To show indifference to the needs of others is in complete contradiction to the teachings of Christ.

In Jesus' day, many assumed that by obeying the commandments, they could show themselves worthy of God's blessings (**Galatians** 3:2). However, Jesus made it very clear that love was a natural result of God's blessing, not a pre-condition for it. The commandment to love is an expression of how Christ's disciples should act. The disciples were commanded to love in the same sense that branches were "commanded" to bear fruit (**John 15:4**).

BIBLE LEARNING

AIM: Students will see Jesus' selfless love as the highest model of friendship and the opposite of the evil example of Cain.

I. OPERATING IN LOVE (1 John 3:11–20)

Caring for others in accordance to God's will usually means doing the opposite of what is favorable in the eyes of the world. Some may retaliate against our good works, especially if our deeds glorify and illuminate the righteousness of Christ. Showing love toward another person should be prompted by genuine sincerity. In these Scriptures, Cain's reaction to God's rejection was murderous intent. An unchecked attitude of anger, jealousy, and hatred can harden the heart, making it implacable. Our harsh words may not result in a person's death; however, words and actions can assassinate someone's character and destroy their self-esteem.

Love and Obedience (verses 11–20)

11 For this is the message that ye heard from the beginning, that we should love one another.

In this verse, John states that love should not be an afterthought. Obedience to Jesus' command to love one another as He loves us is expected of anyone who accepts the Gospel message. Love shows us that the Gospel includes both the benefits of salvation and the responsibility of Christians to love one another. It goes hand in hand and is not separate or tangential to the Christian faith. Love is the message of the Christian faith, obedience to the command and imitation of the life of Jesus Christ.

12 Not as Cain, who was of that wicked one, and slew his brother. And wherefore slew he him? Because his works were evil, and his brother's righteous.

Cain is cited here as an example of one who did not show love for his brother. Cain is characterized as "that wicked one." The word "wicked" (Gk. *poneros*, **poh-ney-ROCE**) is also translated as "hurtful" or "evil" and refers to someone who is bad or would cause harm. John is explicitly saying that Cain belonged to Satan. Saying Cain belonged to Satan is John's way of pointing out that the way we treat each other is part of the larger cosmic battle between good and evil. If we are characterized by love, it will affect our behavior. Likewise, if we are characterized by hatred, it will certainly show in our behavior. Hence the saying that we sin because we are, by nature, sinners. We are not sinners because we sin.

Cain slew his brother Abel because his "works were evil." Notice that same Greek word, *poneros* (**poh-ney-ROCE**), translated earlier in the verse as "wicked one," is now also used to describe the quality of Cain's works. Cain's murderous act was most assuredly not motivated by love, like his brother Abel, but by hatred.

From the example of Cain, we see that hatred facilitates envy, violence, and murder. While we may not literally murder people, we may assassinate their character and reputation because of hatred (cf. **Matthew 5:21–22**). We must avoid hating others, especially Christians, because of the murderous and devilish nature of hatred.

13 Marvel not, my brethren, if the world hate you. 14 We know that we have passed from death unto life, because we love the brethren. He that loveth not his brother abideth in death.

"The world" here is representative of all those opposed to God. John is saying that we as Christians should not be surprised because the world hates us. It is the expectation for Christians to love one another in obedience to Christ's command. Such acts of love, then, translate into acts of righteousness.

Obeying Christ's command to love one another gives Christians an inner knowledge and assurance of their passage from spiritual death to spiritual life. Love for fellow Christians is a dynamic experience that testifies to the reality of the spiritual journey from death to life in Christ. Metaphorically, John compares brotherly love as a rite of passage representative of a significant change or progress in one's spiritual life. It is crucial to note that John does not say that one can pass simply by loving others—that would be salvation by works. Rather, his point is that having love for others is evidence of one's maturity and passage from death of sin to a life based on faith in Christ. So love is the evidence of, and not the means of, salvation.

15 Whosoever hated his brother is a murderer: and ye know that no murderer hath eternal life abiding in him.

This is an echo of Cain's experience from **verse 12**. John presents to his readers the serious consequence of hatred and establishes the parallel between hate and murder: anyone who, like Cain, hates his brother is also a murderer. One could assume that this verse means that a true Christian cannot hate his fellow Christian. But it is a fallacy to believe that the people of God are incapable of hatred and murder.

The Bible records several instances of murder by those who were His people. Moses, who killed an Egyptian (**Exodus 2:12**), and David, who had Uriah killed to conceal his adultery with Bathsheba (**2 Samuel 12:9**), are two major examples. Having established this link with Cain, John now concludes that hatred of others is the spiritual equivalent of murder and that no murderer is entitled to eternal life.

The word for "abiding" is from the Greek word *meno* (**MEH-noh**), which means to remain, last, or endure. Its use here by John is very important. John was saying that although believers possess eternal life, those who hate or murder do not have Christ's Spirit residing within them. Thus, hatred is the equivalent of moral murder.

16 Hereby perceive we the love of God, because he laid down his life for us: and we ought to lay down our lives for the brethren.

The love of God for others is made known not just in words, but in concrete acts of love. The Greek word *ginosko* (**ghin-OCE-koh**), translated here as "perceive," refers to obtaining knowledge. John is saying that we will obtain knowledge of the love of God by looking at the life of Jesus. Very practically, God demonstrated His love to us by sending His Son to lay down His life on our behalf. This demonstration of divine love is the heart of the Gospel. Christ gave His own sinless life to pay the penalty incurred by our sins. He now offers the pardon resulting from this sacrificial act of love to all who will accept it by faith in Him. Divine love is a giving love. God gave His Son for love. The Son gave His life for love. The Greek word *agape* (**ah-GAH-pay**), translated here as "love," finds its ultimate definition in Jesus' unconditional act of giving.

If Christians follow this model of divine love, then they too ought to give something of themselves to express their love for one another. Jesus says, there is no greater love than this self-sacrificing love (**John 15:13**). That is why Christians are called to a self-sacrificing love rather than a self-preserving love. As beneficiaries of this kind of love, it is incumbent on us to love others in the same way.

17 But whoso hath this world's good, and seeth his brother have need, and shutteth up his bowels of compassion from him, how dwelleth the love of God in him?

John says when anyone has the material means to help the needy but refuses to give compassionately, the existence of a Christ-like love in such a Christian is open to question. Using a rhetorical question, John shows that God's love does not exist in anyone who can refuse to help those in need. At issue is not whether God loves the person, but whether such a person possesses God's kind of love toward others. Our material possessions are not given to us only for self-indulgence. God's command to love others requires that we use our possessions to obey that command. Some regard worldly possessions as an end in themselves. But John says they are a means for expressing God's love in us, opening the door of compassion in us, enabling us to reach out to others in need.

The Greek word *splagchnon* (**SPLANGKH-non**) literally means "bowels" or "intestines," but figuratively means "tender mercy or inward affection" and here indicates that compassion is a quality of one's inner emotions. Now, we use similar metaphors when we talk about feeling something deep down, in our "gut," or with our heart. As such, love must unlock it from inside before it can show outwardly. Anybody can perceive a need, but not everybody has the compassion to help others.

18 My little children, let us not love in word, neither in tongue; but in deed and in truth.

Addressing his readers as children not only suggests that John was advanced in years, but also shows the family atmosphere he was trying to create among his readers. There is no better institution that reflects the kind of sacrificial love John is writing about than the family. Including himself in the admonition, he says, "let us not love in word, neither in tongue." The construction suggests like a father giving advice, John was asking them to stop merely talking about love, but show it in deed and truth.

Christian love is more than a feeling: It involves the essential ingredient of giving. Many times when people say they love another, their only real action is from their mouth (i.e., "in tongue"). An expression of love that is backed up by only the tongue is not true love like Christ's self-sacrificing love. True love engages in actions centered on others. The world is tired of passive love; only active love will attract outsiders and make them want to join God's family.

19 And hereby we know that we are of the truth, and shall assure our hearts before him.

The word "hereby" *houtos*, (**HOO-tose**), here meaning "by this" refers to verse 18 and points to an active expression of love that corresponds to Christ's self-sacrifice. When Christians demonstrate this kind of active love, they know they belong to the "truth" (Gk. *aletheia*, (**ah-LAY-thay-ah**), what is true in things pertaining to God and the duties of man, morality, and religious truth). In the parable of the

sheep and the goats, the sheep on Christ's right were commended for their acts of love toward others and were rewarded accordingly by Christ (**Matthew 25:31–46**). In the future, when Christ returns, we will all stand before Him to be judged and rewarded according to our deeds.

20 For if our heart condemn us, God is greater than our heart, and knoweth all things.

The Greek word *kardia* (**kar-DEE-ah**) refers to the heart organ, but here it figuratively denotes the center of all physical and spiritual life. Therefore, if the testimony of our hearts is negative, then we have not been sacrificially reaching out to love others like Christ. Fortunately, God is greater than our hearts and knows better than us our motives for service. The Greek word for "condemn" is *kataginosko* (**ka-ta-gi-NOH-skoh**), which means to find fault, blame, accuse, or condemn. Our motives may be unknown to others, but deep inside we know our reasons. Just as we cannot deceive ourselves, we cannot deceive God, who knows all things.

QUESTIONS 1 & 2

What proves that we have passed from death to life (**v. 14**)?

What shows that we love one another (**vv. 18–20**)?

II. MOTIVATED BY LOVE (vv. 21–24)

When our actions are motivated by love, we can approach God in boldness and confidence. Pure intentions glorify and please God, and a clean heart gives room for His love to flourish. When genuine love occupies our hearts, prayers that encompass both personal and community needs are expressed. These kinds of prayers include fellow Christians, our nation, the church, and the less fortunate. God answers prayers from hearts willing to see the fulfillment of His Word in both private and public arenas.

Love One Another (verses 21–24)

21 Beloved, if our heart condemn us not, then have we confidence toward God. 22 And whatsoever we ask, we receive of him, because we keep his commandments, and do those things that are pleasing in his sight.

As Christians, we must learn to listen to our inner voice so we can have confidence before God. The Greek word for "confidence" is parresia (**par-ray-SEE-ah**), which means openness, or speaking or acting without concealment. It may be easy to deceive others, but God knows our hearts. Therefore, John says, if our hearts are open and honest, we can go confidently before the throne of grace and petition God.

Verse 22 discusses the benefits of a positive testimony of the heart. If we have a confident heart because we keep God's commandments and do the things that please Him, then we also have assurance that we shall receive whatever we pray for that is in line with His will. John's point is that disobeying Christ's command to love can hinder our prayers, so we should obey Him.

23 And this is his commandment, that we should believe on the name of his Son Jesus Christ, and love one another, as he gave us commandment.

In this verse, John provides the crux of his epistle. When Christians act in obedient, self-sacrificing love, we gain confidence toward God. Faith in Christ and love for one another bring us into a new relationship with God where we become His children. Believing on the name of Jesus Christ includes accepting the fact that He is the Son of God who gave His

life to pay the penalty for our sins, reconciling us back to God.

The second part of the commandment is to love one another. The sequence is important. The command is that we both have faith in Christ and also love one another. Faith in Jesus Christ is the basis of our new relationship with God, and love for one another is the expression of that saving faith in us.

24 And he that keepeth his commandments dwelleth in him, and he in him. And hereby we know that he abideth in us, by the Spirit which he hath given us.

To keep God's commands, which includes loving one another, is to abide in Him and to have Him abide in us. As referenced previously in verse 15, the word "abideth" (Gk. meno, **MEH-noh**) means to continually be present. This mutual indwelling characterizes the relationship between God and His Son Jesus and points to their unity (**John 17:21**). The believers' mutual indwelling with God is also a reference to the familial union between God and His believing children.

God is present in believers through His Holy Spirit, who dwells in them (cf. **Romans 8:9, 11**). Through the presence of the Holy Spirit within believers, they have a sense of belonging in God's family. Paul says, "For ye have not received the spirit of bondage again to fear; but ye have received the Spirit of adoption, whereby we cry, Abba, Father" (**Romans 8:15**). This context shows that by the Spirit we know we are children of God (**Romans 8:16**).

BIBLE APPLICATION

AIM: Students will value the abiding nature of God's presence.

Tragedy dominates media attention. The more horrific the crime, the more news coverage it receives. With this kind of media frenzy, wickedness appears to have taken an exalted position in our society, leaving many to question the true value of love. It is no wonder so many of us feel love is trivial and irrelevant. Yet, this lesson tells us no matter what goes on in the world, we are commanded to love one another.

STUDENTS' RESPONSES

AIM: Students will plan ways for believers to express their love for God and others.

Love is a basic human desire and the evidence that we belong to the body of Christ. Love is more than a word, it is a repeated commandment from the Creator: love one another. How can you express love? Make a list of things you can do in your church and community. Volunteer and serve today.

PRAYER

Your sacrifice through Your shed blood, death, and resurrection is true love. Therefore, loving You, Jesus, is a joy that we must treasure. In Jesus' Name we pray. Amen.

DIG A LITTLE DEEPER

The palm branch or frond retains an important role in our Palm Sunday services. When we distribute leaves to the congregation—when we reenact their waving at the time of Jesus' triumphal entry into Jerusalem—we physically partake in this ancient celebration of the Messiah. Palm trees were rich in symbolic significance in the region; this strong and resilient plant represented hope and renewal. Various palm trees bear dates, so palms were also associated with fruitfulness. This explains the cultural significance of palms throughout the world. As plant specialist James Brown tells us in the "Tree Pursuits" website, "Palm trees have been used to symbolize a wide range of different things throughout history, from peace and relaxation to strength and fertility."

The gracefully curved fronds communicate the idea of relaxation and vacation, which is why they are popular symbols in marketing and advertising. Their roots represented stability, as the trees were renowned for withstanding fierce windstorms in the tropics. The tree itself became associated with the concept of victory, "because the palm tree often grows in hard-to-reach places that are difficult to access, making it a symbol of strength and perseverance."

The people of God put this symbolism of the palm tree to good use. "The righteous shall flourish like the palm tree," the psalmist tells us (Ps. 92:12a). It seems impossible for David not to have had the date palm in mind when he wrote, "And he shall be like a tree planted by the rivers of water, that bringeth forth his fruit in his season; his leaf also shall not wither; and whatsoever he doeth shall prosper" (Ps. 1:3). By Solomon's instruction, palm trees were carved as relief on the walls and doors of the Temple (1 Kings 6:29–35). Naturally, the populace in Jesus' day would strew fronds on the ground before a royal procession, or wave leaves in reception of a great personage. Through the symbolism of the palm, the people were paying homage and wishing the king continued success and prosperity. So, too, we wave palm leaves today in church to honor and celebrate our King Jesus!

Ref.: Brown, James. "What Do Palm Trees Symbolize? (The Surprising Meaning Behind Them)." Tree Pursuits (website). https://treepursuits.com/what-do-palm-trees-symbolize/

HOW TO SAY IT

Sacrificial. sa-kri-**FI**-shul.

Bowels. **BOW**-uls.

DAILY HOME BIBLE READINGS

MONDAY
God So Loved the World
(John 3:16–21)

TUESDAY
Love Given Us by God
(1 John 3:1–5)

WEDNESDAY
Loved to the End
(John 13:1–15)

THURSDAY
Great Love Shown
(Luke 7:44–48)

FRIDAY
Those Who Do Not Love
(1 John 3:6–10)

SATURDAY
A New Commandment
(John 13:31–35)

SUNDAY
Love Made Possible by the Spirit
(1 John 3:11–24)

PREPARE FOR NEXT SUNDAY

Read **1 John 4:13–5:5** and study "Believe God's Love."

Sources:

Key Word Study Bible. New International Version. Grand Rapids, MI: Zondervan Bible Publishers, 1996. 1437.

Life Application Study Bible. New International Version. Wheaton, IL: Tyndale House Publishers, 1991. 1909, 2279–80.

The New Oxford Annotated Bible. New Revised Standard Version, New York: Oxford University Press, 2001. 386.

Rainbow Study Bible. New International Version. Grand Rapids, MI: Zondervan Bible Publishers, 1992. 1375.

Tyndale Bible Dictionary. Philip W. Comfort and Walter A. Elwell, eds. Wheaton, IL: Tyndale House Publishers, 2001. 719–728.

Unger, Merrill F. *The New Unger's Bible Handbook*. Chicago, IL: Moody Press, 1998. 634.

COMMENTS / NOTES:

BELIEVE GOD'S LOVE

BIBLE BASIS: 1 John 4:13–5:5

BIBLE TRUTH: Believers are made complete when as a community they abide in God's love and the Spirit of God's love abides in them.

MEMORY VERSE: "Whosoever believeth that Jesus is the Christ is born of God: and every one that loveth him that begat loveth him also that is begotten of him" (1 John 5:1).

LESSON AIM: By the end of the lesson, your students will: comprehend what is required to live in community; talk about experiences of love within the community that exemplify faith and love in God; and celebrate the community's contribution to our formation as disciples of Jesus.

BIBLE BACKGROUND: 1 Corinthians 15:1–22—Read and incorporate the insights gained from the Background Scriptures into your study of the lesson.

LESSON SCRIPTURE

1 JOHN 4:13–5:5, KJV

13 Hereby know we that we dwell in him, and he in us, because he hath given us of his Spirit.

14 And we have seen and do testify that the Father sent the Son to be the Saviour of the world.

15 Whosoever shall confess that Jesus is the Son of God, God dwelleth in him, and he in God.

16 And we have known and believed the love that God hath to us. God is love; and he that dwelleth in love dwelleth in God, and God in him.

17 Herein is our love made perfect, that we may have boldness in the day of judgment: because as he is, so are we in this world.

18 There is no fear in love; but perfect love casteth out fear: because fear hath torment. He that feareth is not made perfect in love.

19 We love him, because he first loved us.

20 If a man say, I love God, and hateth his brother, he is a liar: for he that loveth not his brother whom he hath seen, how can he love God whom he hath not seen?

21 And this commandment have we from him, That he who loveth God love his brother also.

5:1 Whosoever believeth that Jesus is the Christ is born of God: and every one that loveth him that begat loveth him also that is begotten of him.

2 By this we know that we love the children of God, when we love God, and keep his commandments.

3 For this is the love of God, that we keep his commandments: and his commandments are not grievous.

4 For whatsoever is born of God overcometh the world: and this is the victory that overcometh the world, even our faith.

5 Who is he that overcometh the world, but he that believeth that Jesus is the Son of God?

BIBLICAL DEFINITIONS

A. Firstfruits (1 Corinthians 15:20) *aparche* (Gk.)—The best produce, picked first at harvest and usually offered to God; term is also used for people consecrated to God for all time.

B. Resurrection (v. 21) *anastasis* (Gk.)—A rise in status; rising from the dead, specifically that of Christ or all men at the end of this present age.

LIFE NEED FOR TODAY'S LESSON

AIM: Students will better understand how to live in community that is built on unity and mutuality in God's love.

INTRODUCTION

Christian Spiritual Fundamentals

The letters of John are three brief epistles. The succinctness is misleading, for they deal with insightful and significant questions about the fundamental nature of Christian spiritual experience. The Johannine letters also provide fascinating insight to the condition of the church at the end of the first century. Heresy played a critical and deceptive role in the church. Autonomy and church organization are reflected. The genuine nature of a committed and obedient relationship to God through Christ is strongly and affectionately depicted and commanded.

BIBLE LEARNING

AIM: Students will know and understand God's commandments.

I. LIVING PROOF (1 John 4:13–17)

All Christians receive the Holy Spirit as living proof of God's presence in our lives. The Holy Spirit gives us power to love and confess Jesus Christ as Lord, and provides assurance that

we are connected to our Heavenly Father. Perfect love does not mean we love perfectly; it is a description of our Savior's love for us. Jesus loves flawlessly because He accepts us with all our imperfections and mistakes, and regardless of our gender; sex; race; marital, educational, or economic status; physical, mental, or emotional qualities; age; or cultural background. He loves us!

God's Spirit Manifested in Our Lives (verses 13–17)

13 Hereby know we that we dwell in him, and he in us, because he hath given us of his Spirit.

Two themes dominate John's exhortation in **verses 13–21**: faith and love. In **verse 13**, John affirms that the assurance of the presence of God in the life of a Christian (cf. **vv. 12, 15**) is proved by the residence of the Holy Spirit in him or her. Since love is the first of the fruit produced by the Spirit, John's connection of love with the Holy Spirit is obvious, in addition to the other work of the Spirit in the life of a believer.

14 And we have seen and do testify that the Father sent the Son to be the Saviour of the world.

Although no one has seen God, He has revealed Himself visibly in His Son Jesus Christ. As one of the apostolic eyewitnesses, John bears testimony to this fact (cf. **1:1–3**). The Greek word *soter* (**soh-TAYR**), which means savior or deliverer, defines both the purpose and the result of Christ's mission (cf. **Matthew 1:21; John 1:29**).

15 Whosoever shall confess that Jesus is the Son of God, God dwelleth in him, and he in God.

Emphasis is placed on the test of (doctrinal) faith in Christ as evidence of God's indwelling. The Greek word *homologeo* (**ho-mo-lo-GEH-oh**, confess) indicates that confession involves the intellectual acknowledgment of the human-divine nature of Christ and a personal acceptance of Him.

16 And we have known and believed the love that God hath to us. God is love; and he that dwelleth in love dwelleth in God, and God in him.

John effectively connects faith with works (action). Belief must find expression in behavior. Here, believing and loving are intimately joined. They are proof of God's Spirit in the believer.

17 By this is love perfected with us, so that we may have confidence for the day of judgment, because as he is so also are we in this world.

By dwelling in love and consequently in God, and by God dwelling in us, love will be perfected *teleioo*, (**teh-lay-OH-oh**), to complete or accomplish). This word refers to completion of a goal or maturity. Love will be made complete, mature, and perfect once for all in us. This perfection refers to a complete, fully accomplished state. John is stating that the on-going action of God abiding in us and we abiding in God perfects our love. The phrase "because as he is so also are we in this world" refers to God's abiding in us (**v. 16**). If we abide in God and God in us, despite being in this imperfect world, we are like God, who is love. This should give us confidence on the day of judgment which comes from loving as Jesus loved us. It does not mean that we will love perfectly, but that we will have evidence that we are believers, and we will have confidence that our hearts are right before God.

QUESTIONS 1 & 2

How do we know God lives in us (**v. 13**)?

What gives proof that we love God (**vv. 16–17**)?

II. LOVING PROOF (vv. 18–19)

The love of God eradicates all fear. If we operate from fear, it is a sign that we have not fully grasped the concept of God's unconditional love. Even many Christians function in fear and live as prisoners of anxiety, even though the Lord cannot use us when we walk in apprehension. If we fear Judgment Day, are we certain of our salvation? There needs to be a level of confidence in knowing we are saved and eternally secure with Christ.

Love Without Fear (verses 18–19)

18 There is no fear in love, but perfect love casts out fear. For fear has to do with punishment, and whoever fears has not been perfected in love.

John then goes on further to clarify that love is absent of fear. Mature and complete love casts out all fear. The word for "casts out" literally means to lay or throw aside something. Christians should not experience fear of punishment in their life. The punishment that John refers to is the judgment, which is clear because it is mentioned in the context of the day of judgment. Because fear has punishment (the two are inevitably intertwined), the person who fears punishment does not have the love in **vv. 16–17**. The same Greek verb appears again here as "perfect" (*teleioo*), confirming the connection. John seals his point by stating that whoever fears has not matured in love. The one who fears that they will receive the Final Judgment has not experienced the complete work of God's love in their life.

19 We love because he first loved us.

Next we see the motivation behind the Christian's love. It is because we have experienced the love of God in Jesus Christ. This verse points to the detailed description and explanation of the preceding verses. It summarizes what John has said concerning the love of Christ and its effect in the life of a believer. We love God because He has shown His love to us in Christ. We love one another because we have experienced God's love in our hearts.

III. LASTING PROOF (vv. 4:20–5:5)

John's emphasis on loving others is nowhere more clearly reflected than in this passage of Scripture. We are lying if we say we love God, but actually hate our brothers and sisters in Christ. Many biblical teachers skate over these verses because they are too direct. Yet, these verses force us to examine our actions. How can we claim to love the invisible Lord and still be seen to hate the visible inhabitants of His kingdom? We cannot love God apart from loving one another.

Love and Hate (verses 20–5)

20 If anyone says, "I love God," and hates his brother, he is a liar; for he who does not love his brother whom he has seen cannot love God whom he has not seen.

John says that if anyone says they love God and hates their brother, they are more than a walking contradiction: they are a liar. This may not mean they are intentionally deceiving others. At the most basic level, they are deceiving themselves. They are not walking consistent with the truth. Anyone who does not love someone who is physically visible to them cannot love God, who is invisible to their natural senses. For John, the real test of true love is loving those who are right in front of you. Loving people whom you can see is the litmus test of loving the God whom you cannot see.

21 And this commandment we have from him: whoever loves God must also love his brother.

Not only is loving your brother a litmus test for loving God, but not loving your brother is disobedience to the Lord's command. John appeals to the direct command of Jesus (**John 13:34**). If we do not love our brother, we are not obeying the command of Jesus. Jesus has given us this command, and Christians must fulfill it or risk disobeying the Lord who loves them.

1 John 5:1–5

This Scripture passage is a part of John's final elaboration of the three principle tests of authentic Christianity: belief (faith), righteousness (obedience), and love. He has devoted sections of his letter to treating the subjects in turn. Here, all three are closely related, integrated, and woven together into one theological fabric, within the overriding idea of Christian confidence and assurance through the new birth. The text shows the Christian's confidence in victory, witnesses, eternal life, and prayer.

5:1 Whosoever believeth that Jesus is the Christ is born of God: and every one that loveth him that begat loveth him also that is begotten of him.

John connects belief and love mutually and spiritually. The Greek word *pisteuo* (**pihSTEHOO-oh**) means to trust or to believe. It is more than a mere profession of a creed; it means personal faith in and personal union with Christ. Our proof of the new birth is shown as a continual belief in the humanity and deity of Christ and His redemptive mission. The logical consequence of the new birth is an expression of love for God, who is the source of the spiritual birth, as well as to all who have been given birth by Him.

2 By this we know that we love the children of God, when we love God, and keep his commandments.

In the preceding verse, John connects belief and love. In this verse and the next, the connection is made between love and obedience (righteousness), indicating how intertwined the themes are John reverses the relationship by stating that our love for one another is made manifest when we love God and keep His commandments. Previously John declared that we cannot love God if we hate one another. Now John is saying that loving God reveals our love for one another. The two are intimately related, so that both should flow from each other.

3 For this is the love of God, that we keep his commandments: and his commandments are not grievous.

John takes a step further to link love and obedience. This verse is obviously an echo of the precept of Christ Himself: "If ye love me, keep my commandments… He that hath my commandments, and keepeth them, he it is that loveth me…" (**John 14:15, 21**). Love for God is both a basis and motivation for obedience. The Greek word *barus* (**ba-ROOS**), translated as "grievous," also carries the idea of something difficult or burdensome. For example, some of the regulations of the scribes and the Pharisees were heavy burdens hard to bear.

Jesus' yoke, on the contrary, is easy and His burden light (**Matthew 11:30**). Furthermore, divine resources are made available to equip Christians to do the will of God. John directly references the impartation of divine nature and the indwelling presence of the Holy Spirit

in all who have been born of God (see **1 John 3:24**).

4 For whatsoever is born of God overcometh the world: and this is the victory that overcometh the world, even our faith. 5 Who is he that overcometh the world, but he that believeth that Jesus is the Son of God?

John's confidence in the believer's victory is contagious. Within two verses he uses the words "overcome" and "victory" four times (**vv. 4–5**). The Greek verb *nikao* (**nih-KAH-oh**) means to conquer, to overcome, or to prevail, while its related noun *nike* (**NI-kay**) means victory or conquest. Anything that has been born of God conquers the world, but here John focuses on our faith as the victory that has already conquered the world.

Two aspects of the believers' conquest are implied in these verses. First, Christ's victory becomes the believers' own upon their belief in the person and work of Christ, acceptance of Christ as Lord and Savior by faith, and consequent union with Christ (cf. **John 1:12, 16:33**). Second, the abiding presence of the Holy Spirit enables the believer to live in daily victory over the flesh, the world, and the devil. In everyday experience, the Christian can constantly express thanks to God "which giveth us the victory through our Lord Jesus Christ" (from **1 Corinthians 15:57**; cf. **1 John 4:4; Romans 8:37**).

BIBLE APPLICATION

AIM: Students will model their lives after God's love when they love their neighbors.

Society teaches us to love conditionally. Some people live in fear of rejection from those who claim to love them. This is not real love. One of the most remarkable attributes of God is His ability to love unconditionally and completely. No matter what we face in life, God's love is everlasting and nothing can separate us from His love! Not only do we have God's promise of love but also the promise of eternal life. With this kind of reassurance, what keeps us from loving others?

STUDENTS' RESPONSES

AIM: Students will explore different ways that Christians live in God's love in unity and community.

The Lord has high regards for the community of believers, and we should too. All we can do is learn to love and obey God's command. Pray and ask God to reveal where you can extend love to someone in the family of God. After God shows you, act! Write in a journal about how the incident impacted your life and share your experience with the class.

PRAYER

Lord, we pray that we are giving our best in love to others. Help us to learn how and to love one another. Love, faith, and hope are qualities that we should give to one another. In Jesus' Name we pray. Amen.

DIG A LITTLE DEEPER

Paul's introduction to his defense of the doctrine of resurrection seemed to include an early Christian creed (vv. 3–5). Biblical scholarship identifies the technical rabbinic terms, the parallelism, the archaic phrases (e.g., "the third day," "the Twelve"), and other clues that indicate Paul was quoting from an older source. The apostle directly acknowledged that he had "received" and then "delivered" this teaching. We can speculate that Paul was taught the creed when he visited Jerusalem, after spending three years in the Arabian desert (Gal. 1:18,19). We read in the Epistle to

the Galatians that he "went up to Jerusalem to see Peter," and the Greek verb used means 'to gain knowledge of by visiting.' The implication is that those two weeks with Peter and James were a brief training session. Presumably, Paul taught new converts the creed during the year-and-a-half that he resided in Corinth.

The example left by the apostle Paul reminds us of the value of creedal statements for new believers. Memorizing creeds used to be a part of the training that was extended to recent converts. Along with new believers' classes and discipling relationships, creeds were a means of inculcating the doctrines of the church. Creeds tell us what we believe. If we reincorporate memorizing creeds, we may find new believers more secure in the faith.

Ref.: Strobel, Lee. The Case for Easter: a Journalist Investigates the Case for the Resurrection. Grand Rapids, MI: Zondervan, 2003, pp. 65,66.

HOW TO SAY IT

Johannine.	joe-**HA**-nine.
Grievous.	**GREE**-vus.

DAILY HOME BIBLE READINGS

MONDAY
The Holy Spirit Speaks
(Mark 13:5–11)

TUESDAY
Gentiles Receive the Holy Spirit
(Acts 10:39–48)

WEDNESDAY
Full of the Spirit and Faith
(Acts 11:19–26)

THURSDAY
Joy in the Holy Spirit
(Romans 14:13–19)

FRIDAY
Power from the Holy Spirit
(Acts 1:4–8)

SATURDAY
Be Filled with the Spirit
(Ephesians 5:15–21)

SUNDAY
Receive the Holy Spirit
(John 20:19–23)

PREPARE FOR NEXT SUNDAY
Read **Mark 11:1-11** and study "The One Who Comes"

Sources:
International Bible Lesson Commentary. King James Version. Colorado Springs, CO: Dave C. Cook Publishers, 2008.
Key Word Study Bible. New International Version. Grand Rapids, MI: Zondervan Bible Publishers, 1996. 1440–41.
Life Application Study Bible. New International Version. Wheaton, IL: Tyndale House Publishers, Inc., 1991. 1909, 2282–83.
The New Oxford Annotated Bible. New Revised Standard Version, New York: Oxford University Press, Inc., 2001, 386–387.
Rainbow Study Bible. New International Version. Grand Rapids, MI: Zondervan Bible Publishers, 1992. 1378–79.
Tyndale Bible Dictionary. Wheaton, IL: Tyndale House Publishers, Inc., 2001. 719–728.
Unger, Merrill F. *The New Unger's Bible Handbook.* Chicago, IL: Moody Press, 1998. 635–636.

COMMENTS / NOTES:

THE ONE WHO COMES

BIBLE BASIS: Mark 11:1–11

BIBLE TRUTH: Followers of Christ celebrate Jesus' arrival in Jerusalem as the coming of God's kingdom.

MEMORY VERSE: "And they that went before, and they that followed, cried, saying, Hosanna; Blessed is he that cometh in the name of the Lord" (Mark 11:9).

LESSON AIM: By the end of the lesson, your students will: survey the story of Jesus' Triumphal Entry into Jerusalem; discuss their feelings about the kingdom of God; and find creative ways to pay homage to Jesus.

BIBLE BACKGROUND: 1 John 3:11–24; John 11:20–27—Read and incorporate the insights gained from the Background Scriptures into your study of the lesson.

LESSON SCRIPTURE

MARK 11:1–11, KJV

1 And when they came nigh to Jerusalem, unto Bethphage and Bethany, at the mount of Olives, he sendeth forth two of his disciples,

2 And saith unto them, Go your way into the village over against you: and as soon as ye be entered into it, ye shall find a colt tied, whereon never man sat; loose him, and bring him.

3 And if any man say unto you, Why do ye this? say ye that the Lord hath need of him; and straightway he will send him hither.

4 And they went their way, and found the colt tied by the door without in a place where two ways met; and they loose him.

5 And certain of them that stood there said unto them, What do ye, loosing the colt?

6 And they said unto them even as Jesus had commanded: and they let them go.

7 And they brought the colt to Jesus, and cast their garments on him; and he sat upon him.

8 And many spread their garments in the way: and others cut down branches off the trees, and strawed them in the way.

9 And they that went before, and they that followed, cried, saying, Hosanna; Blessed is he that cometh in the name of the Lord:

10 Blessed be the kingdom of our father David, that cometh in the name of the Lord: Hosanna in the highest.

11 And Jesus entered into Jerusalem, and into the temple: and when he had looked round about upon all things, and now the eventide was come, he went out unto Bethany with the twelve.

BIBLICAL DEFINITIONS

A. Laid down (1 John 3:16) *tithemi* (Gk.)—To place, to put, to set or appoint.

B. Beloved (v. 21) *agapetos* (Gk.)—Dearly loved one.

LIFE NEED FOR TODAY'S LESSON

AIM: Students will celebrate God's victory in Christ on a daily basis.

INTRODUCTION

The Journey into Jerusalem

Jesus and His disciples journeyed to Jerusalem for the upcoming Passover. At this point in Jesus' earthly ministry, whenever He went, crowds gathered, curious about the miracles He has performed. During one such stop, a few Pharisees in the crowd questioned Jesus about divorce to trap Him, but instead He clarified the issue for them. He later gave private teaching on divorce to the disciples. As Jesus and the disciples continued to journey on, parents brought their children to Him for a blessing, and a rich man approached, inquiring what he should do to gain eternal life. Once they reached the direct road to Jerusalem, Jesus pulled the twelve aside and predicted His death a third time. James and John requested to be leaders in Jesus' kingdom, but He taught them all that in His kingdom, the leader must serve all. Finally, Jesus healed blind Bartimaeus who sat on the road just outside of Jericho. Once healed, he joined the crowd that had been following Jesus to Jerusalem.

BIBLE LEARNING

AIM: Students will accept Jesus as the ruler of a spiritual realm and believe they are part of the spiritual realm.

I. SUPERNATURAL KNOWLEDGE CONFIRMED (Mark 11:1–6)

Jesus and His disciples were finally within reach of Jerusalem as they approached Bethphage and Bethany at the Mount of Olives. Instead of continuing, He stopped and sent two disciples ahead to find a colt, or young donkey. At this moment in the story, Jesus is poised to reveal a crucial fact about Himself. Perhaps He is very detailed with His instructions because those currently with Him and those who would read of Him later would need to understand that these details

revealed His identity. Saying the colt would be tied speaks to Jesus' identity because it mirrors one of the earliest Messianic prophecies: "The scepter will not depart from Judah, nor the ruler's staff from his descendants, until the coming of the one to whom it belongs, the one whom all nations will honor. He ties his foal to a grapevine, the colt of his donkey to a choice vine" (**Genesis 49:10–11**, NLT).

The Preparation Begins (verses 1–6)

1 And when they came nigh to Jerusalem, unto Bethphage and Bethany, at the Mount of Olives, he sendeth forth two of his disciples,

Jesus and the disciples arrive at Bethphage and Bethany. These two villages were a Sabbath day's journey (approximately 1,000 yards) from Jerusalem. It was a fitting staging point for Jesus' next act of ministry. The Mount of Olives held a special significance in the history of Israel. It was the place that David fled to when Absalom took over Jerusalem. This same place would be the launching pad for Jesus' entry to Jerusalem as its rightful King and Lord. He would not conquer with an army, but with His death on the Cross and subsequent Resurrection. Now it was time for Jesus to enter Jerusalem and fulfill what was spoken about Him in the Old Testament.

The Greek word *apostello* (**ah-poh-STELL-oh**), "sendeth," denotes the sending of a messenger with a special task or commission, and full authority. The disciples were sent as ambassadors with a precise message, speaking in the name of their Master. They were not going in their own authority, but that of Jesus. Their mandate is described in the next verse. Jesus sent the two in order to accomplish a prophecy from **Zechariah 9:9**, thus giving this event messianic significance.

2 and saith unto them, Go your way into the village over against you: and as soon as ye be entered into it, ye shall find a colt tied, whereon never man sat; loose him, and bring him.

The Greek word *polos* (**POH-lahss**) means a young colt. The description of the young animal as one "whereon never man sat" is significant in the light of many Old Testament passages. Animals that were unyoked and unused were sometimes consecrated to a unique and holy use (see **Numbers 19:2; Deuteronomy 21:3; 1 Samuel 6:7**). This animal was fitting to be the one the Messiah would ride on as He entered Jerusalem. In Western countries, the donkey is considered to be stubborn and dumb. However, in the Middle East, the

donkey is considered to possess the qualities of patience, intelligence, and submission. It was also ridden by royalty and nobility. The donkey was usually mounted during peacetime, as opposed to a horse mounted and used during times of war. We read of the prophet Balaam riding on a donkey (**Numbers 22:21**) and of the seventy sons of the judge Abdon riding on seventy donkeys (**Judges 12:13–14**). It was the animal used for nobility in peacetime and also for those who stood in the office of judge. Jesus chose an animal that fit into the bigger picture of His role as Messiah. He was coming as a King but with a different kind of kingdom. His kingdom was a kingdom of peace, not war. He would ride into Jerusalem not as a conquering lion, but the Prince of Peace.

What is also fascinating is Jesus' knowledge of the age and location of the colt. This event was not only messianic but supernatural. By describing the colt and predicting that it would be given to Him, Jesus exercised the wisdom and knowledge from the Holy Spirit.

This foreknowledge of the location and age of the colt would be seen as further proof that Jesus truly is the Messiah. The disciples would definitely be amazed at finding the young donkey in the right location and condition, unused. In their minds this would have solidified Jesus' claim to being Messiah. Here, Jesus is acting as the now reigning King of the Jews, and His prophetic insight into how to fulfill this symbolic act supported that claim, and confirmed to the disciples that God was confirming this claim as well.

3 And if any man say unto you, Why do ye this? say ye that the Lord hath need of him; and straightway he will send him hither.

The Greek word *kurios* (**KOO-ree-ose**), meaning "Lord," refers to Jesus Himself, showing His supreme authority over all things. In any case, Jesus armed His two emissaries against possible difficulties by furnishing them with what to say. He predicted that they would send the animal promptly after the disciples gave this answer. The colt is already under the authority and ownership of the Lord, who now needed him.

4 And they went their way, and found the colt tied by the door without in a place where two ways met; and they loosed him. 5 And certain of them that stood there said unto them, What do ye, loosing the colt? 6 And they said unto them even as Jesus had commanded: and they let them go.

Jesus' ambassadors found the young animal exactly as He had said. It was outside the house and fastened by the door. Precisely what Jesus said would happen did happen. The two disciples wasted no time and loosed the colt. They were obedient to their Master and probably were encouraged by seeing the colt exactly as described. They did encounter some difficulty as some nearby people—the owners or villagers—questioned them regarding the colt. The people were satisfied with the disciples' answer probably because Jesus was well-known for His miraculous deeds and for teaching with authority (see **John 7:46; Mark 11:18**). They knew that this Master could be trusted. They might even have been proud that He wanted to use the young colt.

QUESTION 1

What were Jesus' instructions for finding the colt (**Mark 11:2–3**)?

II. THE PROMISED ONE COMES (vv. 7–11)

Jesus sitting on the colt was fulfillment of Messianic prophecy as well (see Zechariah 9:9). Often, Jesus would not reveal His identity (Mark 1:34, 7:36, 8:26, 11:33), but now His actions declared that He is the Messiah. The people treated Him as a king by throwing their garments on the road (cf. 2 Kings 9:13). They also showed that they recognized that He was not just any king, but rather the One promised to save, by laying down palm branches on the road and shouting the praise word "Hosanna" (Save now! or Please save us!). This is reminiscent of the Feast of Tabernacles, during which this praise is said with the waving of palms. In the context of this holiday, "Hosanna" means salvation is coming, and in the context of Jesus' entry, the Messiah is here. Victory is imminent. To further emphasize that the crowd believed Jesus was the Messiah, the people shouted, "Blessed is he that cometh in the name of the Lord: Blessed be the kingdom of our father David, that cometh in the name of the Lord: Hosanna in the highest" (Mark 11:9–10). This is part of the Hallel praise taken from Psalm 118:25–26, which is spoken during Passover and Pentecost holidays as well as the Feast of Tabernacles.

Praise Him! (verses 7–11)

7 And they brought the colt to Jesus, and cast their garments on him; and he sat upon him. 8 And many spread their garments in the way: and others cut down branches off the trees, and strawed them in the way.

The disciples placed their outer garments on the colt in place of a saddle. Jesus sat and began His ride to the gates of Jerusalem. He was met by a spontaneous expression of homage. The crowd provided "a red carpet" for Him, their King. They threw their garments "in the way." The Greek word here, *eis* (**ACE**), meaning "into," denotes that the crowd threw their garments into the way and spread them there for Jesus to ride over. The picture of Christ riding into Jerusalem on a donkey provoked immediate action, as the people were inspired by this show of humility.

The carpeted way was not made of garments only. The crowd also cut down branches off the trees and strewed them on the road. The Greek word *stibas* (**stee-BAHSS**) speaks of a mass of straw, rushes, or leaves beaten together or strewn loosely so as to form a carpet. John's Gospel account speaks specifically of palm branches being spread out and waved (**12:12–13**). This may have come from the memory of Judas Maccabeus, or Judah the Hammer, who lived almost 200 years before Christ. When Judas defeated the Seleucid Empire and gained control of the temple, the crowds celebrated by waving palm branches.

9 And they that went before, and they that followed, cried, saying, Hosanna; Blessed is he that cometh in the name of the Lord

The Greek word Hosanna comes from the Aramaic phrase *Hoshiah na* (**hoh-SHEE-ah NAH**). Its original meaning is a cry for help: "O save" or "Help, I pray," as in **Psalm 118:25**. Coupled with the blessing that follows, as in Mark, it denotes an expression of praise, rejoicing, or greeting. This psalm is one of the Hallel psalms of praise. It is also known as the "Egyptian Hallel" because it praises God's saving act of delivering Israel from Egypt. The

Greek word *eulogeo* (**ehoo-loh-GEH-oh**) or "blessed" means to speak well of or to praise. The blessing is from God, the source of all blessings. He who comes is blessed by the Lord God to whom He belongs. Jesus was "eulogized" by the crowd, which subjected itself to Him and recognized Him as the Messiah (cf. **Psalm 118:26**). Some evidence suggests the phrase "he who comes" refers to the Messiah, especially as one who rides a young donkey's colt (**Genesis 49:10**). The crowd recognized Jesus' riding on a donkey as the fulfillment of the prophecy in **Zechariah 9:9** and **Genesis 49:11**.

This event showed that Jesus was indeed coming as a King and Messiah. Many of the Jewish people were eager for freedom from Roman rule. The garments and branches in the road and the cries of "Hosanna" in the air were the responses of a people who needed and sought a Savior. Jesus' riding into Jerusalem on a donkey is more than just a fulfillment of Messianic prophecy; it was also a symbolic action in the manner of the Old Testament prophets. By riding into Jerusalem on a donkey, He was publicly showing that He was the King the Jews had been waiting for. This act defied the Romans, who had political authority over Palestine at the time. It also defied the local Jewish ruler Herod and the high priests who also ruled alongside Rome.

Many refer to this as the Triumphal Entry, but it was very different from the triumphal entry of a Roman general. The Romans honored generals who had won a complete and decisive victory over a foreign enemy with a "triumph." This consisted of riding into Rome in a parade followed by captured treasure, enemy prisoners, and all of his military units. At the end of the parade, some of the enemy prisoners were ritualistically executed or thrown to wild animals for the crowd's entertainment.

10 Blessed is the coming kingdom of our father David! Hosanna in the highest!"

The crowds understood this entry to be a sign that God was now in charge. The expectation was that the Messiah would rule as a representative of God and that He would come from the line of David. Their cries focused on the kingdom because they understood that this new King would not continue with business as usual. The Jewish expectation of a Messiah was that God would now be King and turn the whole world upside down.

Hosanna means "O save" or "Help, I pray," but this time it is in the superlative: "Hosanna in the highest." The Greek word *hupsistos* (**HOOP-sis-tose**) means to the highest regions or highest degree possible. It is a word that is often used for God as "the Most High." The crowds gave Jesus praise to the highest degree possible. It was praise that was reserved for God. This was a measure of how much the Jewish people were expecting a Messianic Deliverer and how much they believed that right now, Jesus was that Deliverer.

11 And he entered Jerusalem and went into the temple. And when he had looked around at everything, as it was already

late, he went out to Bethany with the twelve.

Jesus goes into the temple and looks around. The reign of the Messiah was intricately bound with the temple, since the temple was a symbol of God's presence on earth. It was fitting for Jesus to go into the temple although He did not cleanse it at the moment. He and the disciples had journeyed for a day uphill and the text says that it was "already late." With this and after so much excitement had been created with His entry into Jerusalem, Jesus decided to conclude His day. So after looking into the temple and inspecting the premises, He and the twelve spend the night in Bethany. Business in the temple would have to wait.

QUESTION 2

What were the people doing and shouting as Jesus entered Jerusalem (**vv. 8–10**)?

BIBLE APPLICATION

AIM: Students will learn to make certain sacrifices for the Lord's sake.

We live in a society that engages in celebrity worship. We spend hundreds of dollars buying tickets to see our star athletes. We camp out for hours to hear our favorite singers. We stand in long lines to get our pictures taken with movie stars. We want to dress and act like celebrities. We love and honor them. However, Jesus is the only One who truly loves us. He loved us so much He suffered, died, and rose again for our salvation. We should strive to live lives that honor Him.

STUDENTS' RESPONSES

AIM: Students will tell others about the kingdom of God and the joy they have found by being part of it.

We often pray for a house, a promotion, or a mate. There is nothing wrong with looking to God to take care of our every need. However, we should not limit Him to what we perceive is important. Jesus came so that we could have eternal life, and for this, we should honor Him. For your daily devotion, ask God to show you ways you can honor Him and whatever He reveals, do it.

PRAYER

Jesus, thank You for giving us eternal life and peace that will last forever. In Jesus' Name we pray. Amen.

DIG A LITTLE DEEPER

Dr. Gene A. Getz—the impactful author and former pastor of Fellowship Bible Church in Plano, Texas—has a vivid metaphor for the challenge we face in trying to practice love of others. Dr. Getz directs our attention to a huge jumbo jet, like the Boeing 747. When fully loaded with passengers, luggage and fuel, those airplanes could weigh 400 tons. Nevertheless, a 747 could lift off a runway and soar like a bird, because of its powerful jet engines and engineering design: "the law of aerodynamics at work through human ingenuity is more powerful than the law of gravity."

The challenge we have loving others is comparable to the challenge a jumbo jet has with its massive weight. By nature, all of us were "slaves to sin" (Rom. 6:16). We were in bondage and incapable of consistently exercising self-sacrificial love (or fulfilling any other of the Lord's commands). But after salvation, we have access to a power comparable to the jet engines that propel an airplane. If we partner with the Holy Ghost, we too will "lift off" to the heights of love and godliness, defying the gravitational pull of sin. "For the law of the Spirit of life in Christ Jesus hath made me free from the law of sin and death" (Rom. 8:2). Walking in the Spirit is the only way to shed our native selfishness and love sacrificially.

Ref.: Getz, Gene A. Serving One Another. Wheaton, IL: Victor Books, 1984, p. 21.

HOW TO SAY IT

Bethphage.   **BAYTH**-fah-gay.

Bethany.   **BE**-tha-nee.

Hosanna.   ho-**ZA**-na.

DAILY HOME BIBLE READINGS

MONDAY
God Judges the Peoples
with Equity (Psalm 67)

TUESDAY
A Righteous God and a Savior
(Isaiah 45:20–25)

WEDNESDAY
God Highly Exalted Him
(Philippians 2:9–16)

THURSDAY
Beware, Keep Alert
(Mark 13:30–37)

FRIDAY
The Coming Son of Man
(Mark 14:55–62)

SATURDAY
The World Has Gone After Him
(John 12:14–19)

SUNDAY
Blessed is the Coming Kingdom
(Mark 11:1–11)

PREPARE FOR NEXT SUNDAY
Read **1 Corinthians 15:1–11, 20–22** and
study "Resurrection Guaranteed."

Sources:
Black, Clifton. "Gospel According to Mark: Introduction and Mark 11:
    1–11 notes." *The Harper Collins Study Bible*. NRSV. San Francisco,
    CA: Harper
Collins Publishers, 2006. 1722–24, 1745–46.
Henry, Matthew. "Mark 11." *Matthew Henry's Commentary on the
    Whole Bible*. Vol. 5: Matthew to John.
Hurtado, Larry W. "Jesus Enters Jerusalem and the Temple."
    Understanding the Bible Commentary Series: Mark. Grand Rapids,
MI: Baker Books, 2011.
Jensen, Richard A. *Preaching Mark's Gospel: A Narrative Approach.*
    Lima, OH: CSS Publishing Co., Inc. 1996. 168–170.
Shanks, Hershel, ed. *Ancient Israel from Abraham to the Roman
    Destruction of the Temple*. Washington, DC: Prentice Hall, 1999.
    286.
Unger, Merrill F. "Festivals: Feast of Booths (or Tabernacles)." *The New
    Unger's Bible Dictionary*. R.K. Harrison, ed. Chicago, IL: Moody
    Press, 1988. 417–421.
----------. "Mark, Gospel of." *The New Unger's Bible Dictionary*. R.K.
    Harrison, ed. Chicago, IL: Moody Press, 1988. 816.
----------. "Palm Tree." *The New Unger's Bible Dictionary*. R.K. Harrison,
    ed. Chicago, IL: Moody Press, 1988. 957–958.
Watson, Richard and Nathan Bangs. *A Biblical and Theological
    Dictionary: Explanatory of the History, Manners, and Customs of
    the Jews, and
Neighbouring Nations*. New York: B. Waugh and T. Mason, 1832. 927.

COMMENTS / NOTES:

RESURRECTION GUARANTEED

BIBLE BASIS: 1 Corinthians 15:1–11, 20–22

BIBLE TRUTH: Jesus' resurrection provided tangible evidence of the possibility of resurrection for those whose identity is formed by Christ Jesus.

MEMORY VERSE: "For as in Adam all die, even so in Christ shall all be made alive" (1 Corinthians 15:22).

LESSON AIM: By the end of the lesson, your students will: explore the meaning of Christ's resurrection; value and appreciate our identity in Jesus Christ; and witness personally and corporately to the resurrection of Jesus Christ.

BIBLE BACKGROUND: 1 John 4–5; Romans 8:31–39—Read and incorporate the insights gained from the Background Scriptures into your study of the lesson.

LESSON SCRIPTURE

1 CORINTHIANS 15:1–11, 20–22, KJV

1 Moreover, brethren, I declare unto you the gospel which I preached unto you, which also ye have received, and wherein ye stand;

2 By which also ye are saved, if ye keep in memory what I preached unto you, unless ye have believed in vain.

3 For I delivered unto you first of all that which I also received, how that Christ died for our sins according to the scriptures;

4 And that he was buried, and that he rose again the third day according to the scriptures:

5 And that he was seen of Cephas, then of the twelve:

6 After that, he was seen of above five hundred brethren at once; of whom the greater part remain unto this present, but some are fallen asleep.

7 After that, he was seen of James; then of all the apostles.

8 And last of all he was seen of me also, as of one born out of due time.

9 For I am the least of the apostles, that am not meet to be called an apostle, because I persecuted the church of God.

10 But by the grace of God I am what I am: and his grace which was bestowed upon me was not in vain; but I laboured more abundantly than they all: yet not I, but the grace of God which was with me.

11 Therefore whether it were I or they, so we preach, and so ye believed.

20 But now is Christ risen from the dead, and become the firstfruits of them that slept.

21 For since by man came death, by man came also the resurrection of the dead.

22 For as in Adam all die, even so in Christ shall all be made alive.

BIBLICAL DEFINITIONS

A. Made perfect (1 John 4:17) *teleioo* (Gk.)—To complete, finish, reach a goal; be fulfilled.

B. Grievous (5:3) *barus* (Gk.)—Heavy, important, savage, and fierce.

LIFE NEED FOR TODAY'S LESSON

AIM: Students will be reminded of the importance of Jesus' life, death, and resurrection in the lives of believers.

INTRODUCTION

Church Issues

Throughout 1 Corinthians, Paul deals with issue after issue. He addressed the divisions in the church (1:10–4:21), sexual immorality including incest (5:1–13) and fornication (6:12–20), marriage and divorce (7:1–40), idolatry (8:1–11:1), and different aspects of public worship (chapters 11–13). In 1 Corinthians 14, Paul addresses the spiritual gifts of speaking in tongues and prophecy. The apostle instructed that the Corinthians should pursue love and the gift of prophecy because it builds up the whole church. Tongues only build up the individual. The only way tongues can edify the church is if the one speaking has the gift to interpret. Paul writes that proper worship will result in even unbelievers admitting, "God is truly here among you" (1 Corinthians 14:25). The chapter ends with Paul describing the proper order of worship. With all of these other issues dealt with, Paul finally launches into explaining the significance of Christ's Resurrection.

BIBLE LEARNING

AIM: Students will experience the effects of God's grace.

I. RESURRECTION CLARIFIED (1 Corinthians 15:1–5)

There were some in the Corinthian church who did not believe in the resurrection of the dead. Paul reminds them that he had already preached the Good News to them and they had, or so it seemed, fully accepted it. He writes, "It is this Good News that saves you if you continue to believe the message I told you—unless, of course, you believed something that was never true in the first place" (1 Corinthians 15:2, NLT).

The Good News (verses 1–5)

1 Moreover, brethren, I declare unto you the gospel which I preached unto you, which also ye have received, and wherein ye stand; 2 By which also ye are saved, if ye keep in memory what I preached unto you, unless you have believed in vain.

The opening of this chapter introduces Paul's concerns and lays the foundation for the argument he develops in the verses that follow. Some in the Corinthian church exalted the spiritual so much that they devalued the physical. Consequently, this path led to denial of bodily resurrection.

Paul begins with what they have in common. Paul uses the Greek word euaggelion (**ehoo-anGHEL-ee-on**), which means good news message or Gospel, to describe what he preached and they in turn received as a means for salvation. They owe their existence as a community of faith to the Gospel he brought them (Fee 1987; Horsley 2011). He warns if they cannot hold on to the same Gospel that saved them, their faith is in jeopardy of being ineffective and producing no fruit.

3 For I delivered unto you first of all that which I also received, how that Christ died for our sins according to the Scriptures; 4 And that he was buried, and that he rose again the third day according to the Scriptures: 5 And that he was seen of Cephas, then of the twelve:

Paul presents the basics of the Gospel by highlighting three points of emphasis: Jesus died, was buried, and rose again on third day, all in accordance with the Scriptures.

This essence of the Gospel was passed down to Paul. It is generally accepted that these verses reflect an early creed. Being of primary importance, he in turn passed it along to the church in Corinth (Fee 1987).

Although Paul covered a wide range of subjects, not everything he discussed was central to the Gospel nor does every instruction carry equal weight. In this passage, Paul highlights the elements of the Gospel message that are critical to the church and its health and vitality.

The death, burial, and resurrection of Jesus are presented as an objective reality. There is a grave, and there were witnesses. It is not merely a spiritual phenomenon.

In addition to misconceptions about the Resurrection, it is likely that the church in Corinth had some misgivings about Paul's authority. Paul grounds his argument in tradition, Scripture, and apostolic authority.

First, he appeals to tradition by referencing an early church creed. Then, he asserts that these things have hapened according to Scripture. Last, he states that Cephas, or Peter, and the twelve can attest to the validity of his claims. The twelve apostles had an especially close relationship with Jesus and a special role in the founding of the church. Perhaps Peter was singled out because he had followers in the church of Corinth.

QUESTION 1
What is the Gospel message (**1 Corinthians 15:3–4**)?

II. RESURRECTION WITNESSED (vv. 6–11)
Paul offers even more validity to the resurrection by listing the witnesses. Peter and the Twelve saw the resurrected Jesus (John 20:19–29). They had been chosen to be witnesses (Acts 10:40–43). More than five hundred of His followers saw Jesus, including James, Jesus' brother and other apostles (Luke 24:33, 36–53). Perhaps a criterion for being an apostle, from Paul's perspective, was that one had to have been divinely chosen to see the resurrected Christ. They were sent out to preach the Gospel because they could personally testify to its truth (Soards).

Eyewitness Accounts (verses 6–11)
6 After that, he was seen of above five hundred brethren at once; of whom the greater part remain unto this present, but some are fallen asleep. 7 After that, he was seen of James; then of all the apostles. 8 And last of all he was seen of me also, as of one born out of due time.

Paul continues to build the credibility of his position by adding an additional source of authority-eyewitness testimony of believers, apostles, and him. Paul affirms that Jesus was seen by a number of people in a variety of settings after his burial, more than 500 believers, according to Paul. Many of the witnesses were still alive at the time of the writing and their accounts could be verified first hand, although some had already "fallen asleep," a common euphemism at the time for death.

Next Paul says that the resurrected Jesus was seen by James, Jesus' half-brother. He was also a major leader in the Jerusalem church. This would have given Paul even more credibility, as James had major influence with the church at large due to his natural relation to Jesus. Paul also speaks of the resurrected Jesus being seen by the apostles. This is obviously not the twelve because they were just mentioned in verse 5. Paul must have been referring to others outside of the twelve who had been commissioned to represent Christ, perhaps those mentioned in Luke 10:1–20.

Paul establishes a connection between the apostolic tradition and himself, even though there is no evidence he was regarded as one of the Twelve. He is likely referring to his encounter with the risen Lord on the road to Damascus. Paul uses the Greek word ektroma (**EK-troh-ma**), which is often translated abnormally born, to describe his apostolic calling. The Twelve had years of mentoring and close relationship with Jesus during His time on earth. Paul, however, did not become an apostle this way. He may have been expressing feelings of being born out of season since his apostolic calling was out of the ordinary.

9 For I am the least of the apostles, that am not meet to be called an apostle, because I persecuted the church of God. 10 But by the grace of God I am what I am: and his grace which was bestowed upon me was not in vain; but I labored more abundantly than they all: yet not I, but the grace of God which was with me. 11 Therefore whether it were I or they, so we preach, and so ye believed.

Paul explains that he is "least" of the apostles because he formerly persecuted the church. He is unworthy of the calling, and did nothing to earn it. His standing before God as the "least" of the apostles and later as the "chief" of sinners provide the foundation for his deep experience of the grace of God in Jesus Christ.

The grace Paul discusses is best understood as twofold: saving and empowering. By the saving grace of God, Paul was transformed from an enemy of God and the church to a friend. His faith flourished and he was empowered to bear fruit. Paul mentions he "labored more abundantly" than all the Twelve. Grace should not be confused with meritorious effort, as indicated by his assertion that the agent of these works is "yet not I, but the grace of God which was with me." Hard work is not the means of achieving results in his ministry, but a manifestation of God's empowering grace.

The language he uses in verse 11, "I or they," hints that there was debate in the Corinthian church about the authority of various itinerant apostles. He ties what he preached to their faith and all apostles, suggesting it is commonly accepted by all believers. His point is that they all preached the same thing! It allows him to show they were departing from the Gospel message and traditional sources of authority for the church, not him.

QUESTION 2
How does Paul describe himself (**vv. 8–9**)?

III. RESURRECTION GUARANTEED (vv. 20–22)
In verses 12–19, Paul refutes the people's belief that there is no resurrection of the dead with a line of reasoning that in essence concludes that

if there is no resurrection, Christ did not rise and their faith would be useless. They would all still be in their sin, condemned forever. However, Paul reassures his audience, that indeed Jesus had risen from the dead.

THE BENEFITS OF THE RESURRECTION (verses 20–22)

20 But now is Christ risen from the dead, and become the firstfruits of

them that slept. 21 For since by man came death, by man came also the resurrection of the dead. 22 For as in Adam all die, even so in Christ shall all be made alive.

Paul emphasizes the benefits of the resurrection for believers. Christ's resurrection made the resurrection of the dead necessary and inevitable. God raised Christ from the dead based on His own authority and sovereignty. It is required for the final victory over death so God can be "all in all".

Paul uses the Greek word aparkhe (**ah-par-KHAY**), meaning a sacrifice of the harvest's firstfruits to sanctify the whole harvest, to describe the work of Christ. He is the first fruit of a larger harvest (2 Thessalonians 2:13, NIV; 1 Corinthians 16:15, KJV). This agricultural metaphor has eschatological significance, Christ's resurrection is not bound to one annual harvest, but it sanctifies the resurrection of all believers for eternity. For this to happen, Christ had to be human because death is a part of humankind, not God. Christ reversed what Adam set in motion, ushering in a new order. New life and resurrection for believers is inevitable because we share in the new nature of the Resurrected Christ through the grace of God.

QUESTION 3
How do Jesus and Adam differ (vv. 21–22)?

BIBLE APPLICATION

AIM: Students will value the scriptural record of eyewitness testimony.

Certain events define our identities. On the wedding day, we become a spouse. Giving birth to a child, we become a parent. We cherish these life-changing events and commemorate them every year with anniversaries and birth-day celebrations. As believers, another event that deserves our devotion is the Resurrection of Christ. The Resurrection is the foundation of our faith. It is the fuel that motivates us to want to live right and treat others with love and kindness. Without it, we would be eternally lost. Let's remember to celebrate the Resurrection not just once a year, but everyday of our lives.

STUDENTS' RESPONSES

AIM: Students will expand their opportunities to personally identify with Christ as they share the good news of the love of Christ with others.

We love to celebrate life-changing events with others. We book banquet halls a year in advance and hire the best caterers so people can spend a few hours with us on our special day. The greatest event to ever happen to us is the Resurrection, and we should find ways to share it. Pray about at least three people with whom you can share the Good News and create a special occasion for the sharing. For example, meet for breakfast, schedule time at the gym, or invite them to a church function.

PRAYER
Thank You and bless You, our wonderful Lord and Savior. Thank you for sacrificing Your life so that we are forgiven of our sins, and have eternal life. In Jesus' Name we pray. Amen.

DIG A LITTLE DEEPER
We Saints have a built-in platform to practice the lesson we have learned about love. As members of local churches and in fellowship with other believers, we can rehearse acts of love and good works. The church is an excellent testing ground; there can be many hurting people to comfort, a cluster of emotional traps to circumnavigate,

and plenty of temptations to overcome. The average local congregation is well-designed to exercise our faith muscles and teach us about grace and mercy!

We may not realize it, but how we interact with one another as fellow Saints is all-important. It is a witness to the world and a confirmation to ourselves of the change Christ wrought in our lives. And nothing belies the power of God more than discord and resentment within the body of believers. That is why it is crucial for us to practice and ultimately master loving others in the house of God. Let us commit to making our local churches the places where we learn to be agents of agape.

HOW TO SAY IT

Apostolic.　　　　ah-po-STOL-ik.

Eschatological.　　es-ka-to-LAH-gi-cal.

DAILY HOME BIBLE READINGS

MONDAY
Jesus Has Died
(Matthew 27:45–50)

TUESDAY
Christ Has Risen
(Matthew 28:1–8)

WEDNESDAY
Christ Will Come Again
(1 Thessalonians 4:13–18)

THURSDAY
The Resurrection and the Life
(John 11:20–27)

FRIDAY
The Hope of Eternal Life
(Titus 3:1–7)

SATURDAY
If Christ Has Not Been Raised
(1 Corinthians 15:12–19)

SUNDAY
In Fact, Christ Has Been Raised
(1 Corinthians 15:1–11, 20–22)

PREPARE FOR NEXT SUNDAY

Read **2 John** and study "Watch out for Deceivers."

Sources:

Keener, Craig S. The IVP Bible Background Commentary: New Testament. Downers Grove, IL: InterVarsity Press, 1993. 647–650, 670–671.

Lane, William L. Hebrews 9–13. Word Biblical Commentary, Vol. 47B. Dallas, TX: Word Inc., 1991.

Life Application Study Bible. King James Version. Wheaton, IL: Tyndale House Publishers, Inc., 1997. 2154–55, 2170–72.

Radmacher, Earl D., ed. Nelson's New Illustrated Bible Commentary: Spreading the Light of God's Word into Your Life. Nashville, TN: Thomas Nelson Publishers, 1999. 1648–53.

Furnish, Paul Victor. "First Letter of Paul to the Corinthians: Introduction and 1 Corinthians 15:1–11; 20–22 notes." The Harper Collins Study Bible. NRSV. San Francisco, CA: Harper Collins Publishers, 2006. 1932–34, 1952–53.

Soards, Marion L. "Back to the Basics: 1 Corinthians 15: 1-11."

Understanding the Bible Commentary Series. Grand Rapids, MI:
Baker Books. 2011.

Unger, Merrill F. "Corinth." The New Unger's Bible Dictionary. R.K.
Harrison, ed. Chicago, IL: Moody Press, 1988. 255–256.

----------. "1 Corinthians." The New Unger's Bible Dictionary. R.K.
Harrison, ed. Chicago, IL: Moody Press, 1988. 256.

----------. "Paul." The New Unger's Bible Dictionary. R.K. Harrison, ed.
Chicago, IL: Moody Press, 1988. 968–969.

COMMENTS / NOTES:

WATCH OUT FOR DECEIVERS!

BIBLE BASIS: 2 John

BIBLE TRUTH: Believers who remain faithful in their belief in Christ will have eternal life; and beware of deceivers who will corrupt the community of believers.

MEMORY VERSE: "Look to yourselves, that we lose not those things which we have wrought, but that we receive a full reward" (2 John 8).

LESSON AIM: By the end of the lesson, your students will: RESEARCH John's caution to beware of those who do not abide in Christ's teachings; REFLECT on the emotional response to teachings that are contrary to what they have been previously taught; and TESTIFY that walking in Jesus' commandment to love protects the faith community from deceivers and corruption.

BIBLE BACKGROUND: 1 John 5:6–12, 18–20; 2 John; Galatians 6:6–10—Read and incorporate the insights gained from the Background Scriptures into your study of the lesson.

LESSON SCRIPTURE

2 JOHN, KJV

1 The elder unto the elect lady and her children, whom I love in the truth; and not I only, but also all they that have known the truth;

2 For the truth's sake, which dwelleth in us, and shall be with us for ever.

3 Grace be with you, mercy, and peace, from God the Father, and from the Lord Jesus Christ, the Son of the Father, in truth and love.

4 I rejoiced greatly that I found of thy children walking in truth, as we have received a commandment from the Father.

5 And now I beseech thee, lady, not as though I wrote a new commandment unto thee, but that which we had from the beginning, that we love one another.

6 And this is love, that we walk after his commandments. This is the commandment, That, as ye have heard from the beginning, ye should walk in it.

7 For many deceivers are entered into the world, who confess not that Jesus Christ is come in the flesh. This is a deceiver and an antichrist.

8 Look to yourselves, that we lose not those things which we have wrought, but that we receive a full reward.

9 Whosoever transgresseth, and abideth not in the doctrine of Christ, hath not God. He that abideth in the doctrine of Christ, he hath both the Father and the Son.

10 If there come any unto you, and bring not this doctrine, receive him not into your house, neither bid him God speed:

11 For he that biddeth him God speed is partaker of his evil deeds.

12 Having many things to write unto you, I would not write with paper and ink: but I trust to come unto you, and speak face to face, that our joy may be full.

13 The children of thy elect sister greet thee. Amen.

BIBLICAL DEFINITIONS

A. Deceiver (2 John 7) *planos* (Gk.)—An imposter or misleader; seducer.
B. Antichrist (v. 7) *antichristos* (Gk.)—An opponent of the Messiah.

LIFE NEED FOR TODAY'S LESSON

AIM: Students will understand how belief and actions in God's love and eternal life, provides strength and care for believers.

INTRODUCTION

Teach the Truth

In **2 John**, the issue lies with those who do not profess Jesus to be fully human (such as the docetists who thought Jesus' physical form was a phantasm of God). John's second epistle battles this ungodly perspective and the wicked behavior that stems from its teaching. The apostle encourages true believers to keep the faith. He reiterates God's commandment of love and the necessity of walking in love and truth. He gingerly reminds the congregation of his desires to visit them soon. His message is not written in a stern, threatening, supervisory voice, yet is concise and powerful. This epistle is relevant not only to the Johannine Christians, but also to modern-day Christians. To obscure the truth, practice erroneous doctrine, and partner with deceitful instructors violates the fundamental principles of the Gospel. This principle does not originate with the apostle John; it is traceable to an idea Jesus established (**John 3:20–21**).

BIBLE LEARNING

AIM: Students will understand that behavior and belief are interconnected.

I. Walk in Truth (2 John 1–3)

The truth John refers to is the acknowledgment that Jesus Christ is the Son of God, fully human and fully divine; to recognize that Jesus, who is the one true God, came in the flesh so that we can know God, and through Him attain eternal life (**1 John 5:20**).

Love In Truth (verses 1–3)

1 The elder unto the elect lady and her children, whom I love in the truth; and not I only, but also all they that have known the truth; 2 For the truth's sake, which dwelleth in us, and shall be with us for ever. 3 Grace be with you, mercy, and peace, from God the Father, and from the Lord Jesus Christ, the Son of the Father, in truth and love.

John begins this letter with the common introductory greeting of an epistle. He addresses himself as the elder. The recipient is the elect lady. This woman could have been the host or leader of a particular Christian church. John declares his love for her and "her children." This love is qualified by being in the truth. It is not clear whether these are her biological children or children in the Lord. He then states that this love is not particular to him but universal to all who know the truth. This love is motivated by the truth that dwells in all who know it. John here gives personal qualities to "the truth," perhaps as a way to refer to Jesus Christ, who described Himself as "the Way, the Truth, and the Life."

John says this "truth" will be with us forever. It is an eternal truth that lives with them. It is more than just objective facts; it is living, breathing truth. John concludes his introductory greeting with the standard well wishes of grace, mercy, and peace. What distinguishes him from other New Testament writers is that he includes himself in the well wishes. He says this "grace, mercy, and peace will be with us"—the ones who know the truth (**v. 3**). This grace, mercy, and peace is not just from John and does not rest in his mere human words; it comes from God the Father and the Lord Jesus Christ.

II. WALK IN LOVE (vv. 4–6)

The love described in this epistle is not the love portrayed in cinema. It is unconditional love that nullifies selfishness and epitomizes genuine concern for others. We cannot mimic God's love without the sustaining power of the Holy Spirit. John understood that love is a powerful motivation. Our capacity to love is often fashioned by our experiences. John penned declarations about God's loving character because he experienced His love firsthand. He called himself "the disciple whom Jesus loved" (**John 21:20**). Jesus' love is clearly communicated by all the Gospel writers, yet it is more prominent in John's literature. John was sensitive to those words and actions of Jesus that illustrated how the One who is love loved others.

Belief and Actions (verses 4–6)

4 I rejoiced greatly that I found of thy children walking in truth, as we have received a commandment from the Father.

Characteristically as a shepherd, John's heart was highly elated at the consistent Christian life of members of the congregation to whom he wrote. "Walking" here is from the Greek word *peripateo* (**peh-ree-pah-TEH-oh**), which literally means to walk around, and is figuratively used to signify the habits of the individual life. The use of the word "truth" *aletheia*, (**ah-LAY-thay-ah**) implies its doctrinal and ethical denotations. To walk in the truth involves belief and behavior. Walking in the truth conveys the imagery of a path that one walks on and keeps on course without deviating. The tense of the word indicates a perpetual pattern of healthy spiritual life. The truth that John talks about did not originate with

humankind, not even with the apostles themselves, who originally received it. The truth originated in divine revelation, and so is the command (Gk. *entole*, **en-tow-LAY**) to obey it. Indeed, in John's epistle, both the truth and the commandments are synonymous (cf. **vv. 5–6**).

5 And now I beseech thee, lady, not as though I wrote a new commandment unto thee, but that which we heard from the beginning, that we love one another.

John proceeds from commendation to exhortation, based on personal request (Gk. *erotao*, **ehroh-TAH-oh**, to ask, beg, appeal, or entreat). The commandment he affirms and urges on his readers was not new; it was as old as the Gospel (cf. **John 13:34–35**) or the time of their hearing and receiving of the same. Here, the command to believe is added to the command to love. To believe in the full humanity and divinity of Christ and His redemptive mission, and to demonstrate brotherly love, is proof of the new birth (**1 John 4:7, 5:1**).

6 And this is love, that we walk after his commandments. This is the commandment, That, as ye have heard from the beginning, ye should walk in it.

John pursues the line of argument of his first letter—that Christian love is more than emotion; it is action (demonstration). Love for God and Christ is expressed in practical obedience (**John 14:15, 21, 15:10; 1 John 5:2–3**; cf. **Romans 8:8**). Jesus summarized the whole Law in the greatest commandment: love (**Matthew 22:37–40**). Here, John urges a continual walk in love: "that you follow love" (RSV).

In the second part of this message (**vv. 7–11**), John draws the attention of the church to the threat from without: false teaching. He shifts focus from the true believers to the false teachers—from the wheat to the tares (**Matthew 13:24–30, 36–43**). John describes the heretics, identifies their error, and warns to neither be deceived by them nor give any encouragement to them. In this Scripture passage, John commands watchfulness. He urges the believers to remain loyal not only in love, but also to the teaching of Christ.

QUESTION 1

What is the meaning of love (**2 John 6**)?

III. WALK IN OBEDIENCE (vv. 7–13)

False teachers do not walk in obedience to God's truth. Moral irresponsibility, acceptance of sin, and disregard for the spiritual, mental, and emotional welfare of others are common outcomes of fallacious doctrine. John's letter reminds Christians to live ethically, compassionately, and discerningly. To deny the humanity and deity of Jesus Christ is heresy. The apostle warns faithful believers to forfeit all association with false teachers. His message is relevant in our communities today. We should not lend ourselves to opposing philosophies. The company of false teachers allows them to propagate their doctrine and can signify our approval of what they do.

False Teachers (verses 7–13)

7 For many deceivers are entered into the world, who confess not that Jesus Christ is come in the flesh. This is a deceiver and an antichrist.

John affirms the appearance of false teachers in the world. He describes the false teachers as "deceivers" and "an antichrist." The Greek word *planos* (**PLAH-nohs**), translated as "deceiver," implies an impostor or corrupter, signifying wandering or leading astray. This is a repeat of his earlier warning against

"deceivers" and "many antichrists" (**1 John 2:18, 26; 4:1–6**). An antichrist is literally someone who is against the Messiah *anti*, (**ahn-TEE**), against, instead of; *Christos*, (**khreess-TOSE**), Messiah, anointed one). This is not a separate category of people from the deceivers, but instead those who deceive concerning Christ's nature are opposed to Christ and are described with both of these terms. The errors of the heretic are both moral and doctrinal; the latter is in focus here. The Greek word *homologeo* (**ho-mah-lo-GEH-oh**), translated as "confess," also means to acknowledge, admit, or affirm. A heretic denies the incarnation of Christ as fully man and fully deity.

8 Look to yourselves, that we lose not those things which we have wrought, but that we receive a full reward.

This is the first command of the letter: a warning to be on guard. The present imperative of the Greek word, *blepo* (**BLEH-poh**), implies continual watchfulness to prevent disaster. John commands readers to reject the enticement of error for two reasons: to prevent the ruin of what both they and John had worked for, and to ensure that they would be paid their reward in full.

9 Whosoever transgresseth, and abideth not in the doctrine of Christ, hath not God. He that abideth in the doctrine of Christ, he hath both the Father and the Son.

Two contradictory consequences of heterodoxy (or false doctrine) and orthodoxy are stated. The negative is first mentioned. The Greek word *proago* (**pro-AH-goh**), rendered "transgresseth," literally means to lead before. The false teachers were trying to change the core doctrine the Christians had received—he who fails to abide (Gk. *meno*, **MEHN-oh**, to stay or remain) by the doctrine cannot have the Christ and His salvation. The opposite is also true. To remain continually in the doctrine (Gk. *didache*, **dih-dah-KAY**) or teaching of Christ, showing belief in and obedience of the same, is the proof of the believer's personal relationship to both the Father and the Son.

10 If there come any unto you, and bring not this doctrine, receive him not into your house, neither bid him God speed: 11 For he that biddeth him God speed is partaker of his evil deeds.

John adds a practical note after warning about deceivers. He says that the church is not to receive (Gk. *lambano*, **lam-BAH-noh**) these deceivers into their houses. He then goes even further to say that they should not even bid them "God speed" (Gk. *chairo*, **KHEYE-roh**). This is the word for "rejoice" or "be glad." It became a common greeting or salutation that essentially meant to be well.

The reason behind this action toward false teachers is that by receiving them into your home or wishing them well, you partake (Gk. *koinoneo*, **koy-noh-NEH-oh**) in the false teachers' evil deeds.

12 Having many things to write unto you, I would not write with paper and ink: but I trust to come unto you, and speak face to face, that our joy may be full. 13 The children of thy elect sister greet thee. Amen.

John concludes the letter by letting the church know that he has so much he wants to say that he would rather tell them in person. He does not want any confusion or misunderstanding concerning what he says so that "our joy may be full." He includes himself in the experience of having this joy full (Gk. *pleroo*, **play-RAHo**). This word means to be complete or filled to the brim. John and the church's joy will be completed once they talk face to

face. John finally ends with a salutation from the children of the elect sister. These might have been the biological children of a woman related to the elect lady or fellow converts of the church.

QUESTION 2

What are the consequences of wandering from the truth (**vv. 9–11**)?

BIBLE APPLICATION

AIM: Students will affirm that observing the commandments protects the community of faith in love.

Financial scandals, fueled by deception and greed, have crushed the American people's perception on our nation's financial stability. Financial crises caused many to lose their livelihood, sense of security, self-esteem, and dignity. Lives were ruined and many never recovered economically or emotionally. Believing a lie is dangerous and costly. Christ's teaching is in direct opposition to the deception and selfishness that are rampant in our society. Jesus commands that we live in love and honesty. Anyone who claims devotion to Christ must live by these directives.

STUDENTS' RESPONSES

AIM: Students will identify false teachings against the commandments of Christ and ways to respond to these false teachings.

To remain faithful to Jesus' teaching requires tenacity and a commitment to study God's Word. It also means obeying His commandments. We can also help others who do not know the truth through our testimonies and sharing the Good News of the Gospel. Make a decision to share your testimony about how God transformed your life!

LESSON 9 • APRIL 27, 2025

PRAYER
Dear God, open our eyes to false teachings that draw us away from You. Allow us to see and be active participants with Jesus in our hearts, minds, and bodies. In Jesus' Name we pray. Amen.

DIG A LITTLE DEEPER
At the writing of this, it is about a month following the death of Bishop Carlton Pearson, one-time host of the celebrated AZUSA Conferences. He had been licensed and ordained in the Church of God in Christ, but later became a mentee of Oral Roberts and served in the latter's evangelistic association. Pearson's AZUSA meetings were celebrations of Pentecostal culture, and were among the first such major conferences in arenas and convention centers hosted by an African-American minister. In the 1990s, his platform brought attention to many Pentecostal preachers who spoke at AZUSA, including T.D. Jakes, Myles Munroe, Joyce Meyer, and Juanita Bynum, to name a few.

But, of course, Bishop Pearson has a complicated legacy, because of a doctrinal shift in his ministry when he began to promote what he termed "the Gospel of Inclusion." Proposing a type of universalism—that denied eternal punishment and the existence of Hell—he stunned and disappointed the Christian world. Most of the Saints walked away from the megachurch he pastored, and former colleagues shunned the AZUSA conferences. In March 2004, Pearson was labelled "a heretic" by the Joint College of African-American Pentecostal Bishops.

I think of Carlton Pearson as I read through the Second Epistle of John, and meditate upon the apostle's warning not to give encouragement to a false teacher. To a large extent the body of Christ took John's instruction to heart concerning Bishop Pearson.

Of course, in the secular culture he was regarded as a freethinker and a martyr of "intolerant" religion, but we cannot expect the approval of the world when we stand up for biblical doctrine. I recommend an essay by Virgil Walker (referenced below) if you want to learn more about Bishop Pearson's problematic teachings and the response of the Church.

Ref.: Walker, Virgil. "Unraveling the Legacy of Carlton D. Pearson: A Deep Dive," Just Thinking (blog), December 14, 2023.

HOW TO SAY IT
Transgresseth.   trans-**GRESS**-ith.

Beseech.   bih-**SEECH**.

DAILY HOME BIBLE READINGS

MONDAY
They Refuse to Know the Lord
(Jeremiah 9:1–7)

TUESDAY
Don't Listen to Impostors
(Acts 15:22–35)

WEDNESDAY
False Prophets Will Lead Many
Astray (Matthew 24:3–14)

THURSDAY
Avoid Those Who Cause
Dissensions (Romans 16:16–20)

FRIDAY
The Boldness We Have in Christ
(1 John 5:6–15)

SATURDAY
God Protects Those Born of God
(1 John 5:16–21)

SUNDAY
Be on Your Guard
(2 John 1–13)

PREPARE FOR NEXT SUNDAY

Read **3 John** and study "Coworkers with the Truth."

Sources:

Key Word Study Bible. New International Version. Grand Rapids, MI: Zondervan Bible Publishers, 1996. 1442.

Life Application Study Bible. New International Version. Wheaton, IL: Tyndale House Publishers, Inc., 1991. 1909, 2285–87.

The New Oxford Annotated Bible. New Revised Standard Version, New York: Oxford University Press, Inc., 2001. 395–400.

Rainbow Study Bible. New International Version, Grand Rapids, MI: Zondervan Bible Publishers, 1992. 1381

Tyndale Bible Dictionary. Wheaton, IL: Tyndale House Publishers, Inc., 2001. 719–728.

Unger, Merrill F. *The New Unger's Bible Handbook.* Chicago, IL: Moody Press, 1998. 640.

COMMENTS / NOTES:

COWORKERS WITH THE TRUTH

BIBLE BASIS: 3 John

BIBLE TRUTH: Hospitality is one way that Christians express their faith in Christ to others, making the faithful coworkers with the truth.

MEMORY VERSE: "We therefore ought to receive such, that we might be fellowhelpers to the truth" (3 John 8).

LESSON AIM: By the end of the lesson, your students will: learn the importance of hospitality as written in 3 John; tell of experiences of hospitality and the reactions to it; and practice acts of hospitality.

BIBLE BACKGROUND: 3 John; 2 Timothy 2:14–19—Read and incorporate the insights gained from the Background Scriptures into your study of the lesson.

LESSON SCRIPTURE

3 JOHN, KJV

1 The elder unto the wellbeloved Gaius, whom I love in the truth.

2 Beloved, I wish above all things that thou mayest prosper and be in health, even as thy soul prospereth.

3 For I rejoiced greatly, when the brethren came and testified of the truth that is in thee, even as thou walkest in the truth.

4 I have no greater joy than to hear that my children walk in truth.

5 Beloved, thou doest faithfully whatsoever thou doest to the brethren, and to strangers;

6 Which have borne witness of thy charity before the church: whom if thou bring for-ward on their journey after a godly sort, thou shalt do well:

7 Because that for his name's sake they went forth, taking nothing of the Gentiles.

8 We therefore ought to receive such, that we might be fellowhelpers to the truth.

9 I wrote unto the church: but Diotrephes, who loveth to have the preeminence among them, receiveth us not.

10 Wherefore, if I come, I will remember his deeds which he doeth, prating against us with malicious words: and not content therewith, neither doth he himself receive the brethren, and forbiddeth them that would, and casteth them out of the church.

11 Beloved, follow not that which is evil, but that which is good. He that doeth good is of God: but he that doeth evil hath not seen God.

12 Demetrius hath good report of all men, and of the truth itself: yea, and we also bear record; and ye know that our record is true.

13 I had many things to write, but I will not with ink and pen write unto thee:

14 But I trust I shall shortly see thee, and we shall speak face to face. Peace be to thee. Our friends salute thee. Greet the friends by name.

BIBLICAL DEFINITIONS

A. **Fellowhelpers** (3 John 8) *sunergos* (Gk.)—Companions in work, fellow workers.

B. **Truth** (**v. 8**) *aletheia* (Gk.)—Dependability, fidelity; moral and religious truth; what is true in things relating to God and the duties of man.

LIFE NEED FOR TODAY'S LESSON

AIM: Students will really appreciate the kindness and generosity they have experienced because of good hospitality.

INTRODUCTION

John, the Elder

John names himself "the Elder" in his outreach to Gaius. Although not explicit in his epistle, tradition suggests that he is writing from Ephesus. What is clear, however, in this letter is the importance of strong relationships within the early church. Far different from modern Western culture's obsession with individualism and isolation, the world of John, Gaius, and even Diotrephes depended heavily on a network of closely intertwined community connections. While we are able to choose how deeply we will become involved with people different from ourselves, the early church was a blend of people from various walks of life. As John writes this third epistle, his words convey a key element of hospitality, which is genuine appreciation. He is both a spiritual elder in the church, and a physical elder of advanced age. This has earned him a wealth of experience with people at their best and worst.

BIBLE LEARNING

AIM: Students will know that showing hospitality shows truth and encourages others to be coworkers with the truth.

I. The Heart of Hospitality (3 John 1–4)

In John's Gospel and letters, "truth" (Gk. *aletheia*, **ah-LAY-thay-ah**) includes freedom from affectation, pretense, simulation, falsehood, and deceit. Since John greets his friend in the truth, loves him in truth, walks with him in truth, and encourages the church to be cooperative in the truth, we know that truth is at the heart of Christian hospitality (**vv. 1–4**). This recognition of truth may tempt us to say that we should only associate with others who walk likewise in the truth. While it is important that we as believers connect ourselves with others who hold the truth of Christ at heart, we should also be mindful that our Christian obligation is not just to hold the truth secret. Our job as ministers of Christ is to take and share His truth (**vv. 3–4**).

The Truth of Jesus Christ (verses 1–4)

1 The elder unto the wellbeloved Gaius, whom I love in the truth. 2 Beloved, I wish above all things that thou mayest prosper and be in health, even as thy soul prospereth.

John addresses this letter to Gaius, who appears to be a leader in the church. He states his love for Gaius in the same way that he states his love for the elect lady and her children in **2 John**. His love is "in the truth." This is the truth of Jesus Christ. He adds to his well wishes toward Gaius by saying that he wishes "above all things that thou mayest prosper and be in health, even as thy soul prospereth." Many have used this to justify the prosperity teaching that God wants all people to be rich, when in fact this verse does not communicate material prosperity for all. These are actually general well wishes and not a promise from God. John puts these general well wishes in a Christian context by also desiring the prosperity or health of Gaius' soul.

3 For I rejoiced greatly, when the brethren came and testified of the truth that is in thee, even as thou walkest in the truth. 4 I have no greater joy than to hear that my children walk in truth.

John was overwhelmed with joy (twice in two verses) over the report of the balanced spiritual life of Gaius. The first characteristic of the latter's faith is underscored in these verses: he possessed and lived the truth, the fact of which was attested by the external testimony of fellow Christians.

QUESTION 1

What does it mean to walk in the truth (3 John 3)?

II. WORKING TOGETHER REQUIRES WORK (vv. 5–8)

John continues his epistle by providing specific recognition of the hard work Gaius and his congregation have performed. Often in church life we find ourselves giving until it hurts. Sometimes this is financial. Other times, our contributions are in large amounts of time spent or in providing supplies and resources for the work at hand. Still, we are human and it is quite normal for us to feel that our great sacrifices are not recognized. John acknowledges that Gaius' flock is diligent and faithful to the ministers and missionaries they have served. He has received good reports from them and he has firsthand knowledge of their good reputation for superior care (**vv. 5–6**). Knowing that there may be challenges to their ability to provide accommodations, John praises the church for what they have done, confirming their reputation is sure. He reminds them, however, that whatever the cost of their hospitality, it is still no greater than the price Jesus paid for our sins.

Beloved Community (verses 5–8)

5 Beloved, thou doest faithfully whatsoever thou doest to the brethren, and to strangers; 6 Which have borne witness of thy charity before the church: whom if thou bring forward on their journey after a godly sort, thou shalt do well:

The second characteristic of the balanced spiritual life of Gaius is his love, demonstrated practically among Christians, especially in warm and rich hospitality toward Christian missionaries. Such care for missionaries was a great service, particularly at a time when inns and guest houses were scarce and uncomfortable (cf. **Hebrews 13:2**).

Beneficiaries of Gaius' hospitality gave testimonies, confirming the quality of his faith and love publicly in the assembly (Gk. *ekklesia*, **eckklay-SEE-uh**, the church).

He is further encouraged to remain committed to this labor of love. The Greek word *propempo* (**pro-PEHM-poh**), translated "bring forward," indicates that the missionaries are to be provided with necessities and escorts for the next stage of their journey.

The phrase translated "after a godly sort" or "in a manner worthy of God" (NIV) describes the manner in which the traveling missionaries are to be sent on their journey. They are messengers of God, and as such, they are to be treated with the same type of honor that God is worthy of. This is an extraordinary standard of hospitality!

7 Because that for his name's sake they went forth, taking nothing of the Gentiles.

John here offers as examples reasons for encouraging such support. First, the traveling Christians were missionaries:

73

they went out on a Gospel mission. Christ, not money, was their motive. The phrase "for his name's sake" is a common Semitic (or Hebrew) reference to God. Because God's actual name was so holy, Jews would say "the name" rather than "Yahweh" when talking about God. Thus, the verse could be translated "Because that for Yahweh's sake..." Second, they were not "funded" by the Gentiles. They had no means of support other than the Christians.

8 We therefore ought to receive such, that we might be fellowhelpers to the truth.

The pronoun "we" (referring to Christians) is emphatic. The Greek word *opheilo* (**ah-FAY-loh**, "ought") carries a sense of obligation. Christians have the moral duty to actively support the work of God. A third reason is that such support is actually a partnership in the truth.

QUESTION 2
What was significant about acting faithfully toward the brethren and to strangers (v. 5)?

III. CHALLENGES TO THE TRUTH (vv. 9–14)
John boldly calls out Diotrephes (v. 9), who is in church leadership, yet defies the commandment of hospitality. This is a most distressing error that unfortunately can happen even today. Diotrephes represents an even worse threat to the church than the false teachers John warned against in his earlier epistles. As a result, although Diotrephes has taken position and no doubt made himself lord within the church, we should be cautious not to allow our earthly authority to supersede the truth of Christ, which encompasses Jesus' examples and explicit teaching. To call oneself Christian yet refuse hospitality to believers is to commit a disastrous sin. The church needs to reflect God,

who welcomes us all to the table. Diotrephes needed to be a better example like Gaius and Demetrius (v. 12), remembering that despite rank, there is no division in Christ; we are all one (Galatians 3:28).

A True Servant's Heart (verses 9–14)
9 I wrote unto the church: but Diotrephes, who loveth to have the preeminence among them, receiveth us not.

Now John cites a contrast to shun: Diotrephes is the self-seeking church leader who exhibited a bad example. He refused hospitality to delegates from John. He was motivated not by truth and love like Gaius, but by personal ambition.

10 Wherefore, if I come, I will remember his deeds which he doeth, prating against us with malicious words: and not content therewith, neither doth he himself receive the brethren, and forbiddeth them that would, and casteth them out of the church.

Other antitheses of truth and love demonstrated by Diotrephes are listed here. First, he spread slanderous gossip against John. Second, he went from words to action: he refused hospitality to delegates who came from John. Third, he prevented others in the church from entertaining the traveling missionaries. And finally, he expelled those who resisted his authority.

11 Beloved, follow not that which is evil, but that which is good. He that doeth good is of God: but he that doeth evil hath not seen God.

The first command of this letter is contained in this verse. John's exhortation to Gaius in view of the bad example of Diotrephes is expressed negatively and positively. The Greek word *mimeomai* (**mih-MEH-oh-my**) means to use as a model, imitate, emulate, or follow. Negatively, Gaius is to forsake the bad example just cited. The Greek word *kakos* (**kah-KOHSS**) describes what is bad, evil, or harmful. Positively, he is to follow the good model (i.e., Demetrius in the next verse).

The Greek word *agathos* (**ah-gah-THOHSS**) defines what is morally and spiritually good. John also states the reason for his command: A tree is known by its fruit (cf. **Matthew 7:20**). A Christian's behavior is evidence of his or her spiritual condition.

12 Demetrius hath good report of all men, and of the truth itself: yea, and we also bear record; and ye know that our record is true.

There is much speculation on the identity of Demetrius. Some believe he was the one who carried this letter to the congregation. As such, John wanted the local church to give him a good reception. The phrase "hath good report" is a single verb in Greek (*martureo*, **mar-too-REH-oh**, to confirm or testify to). A better translation would be "well spoken of." This verb is in the perfect tense and implies that this good report of Demetrius had been given over a period of time and continued to be up to date. John also adds that not only do people in the church speak well of Demetrius, but his life and teaching is also aligned with the truth of the Gospel itself. To complete the list of Gaius' recommendation, John lets Gaius know that Demetrius is well spoken of by John and the local church. This personal recommendation along with all the others would carry weight in the eyes of Gaius and the recipients of the letter.

13 I had many things to write, but I will not with ink and pen write unto thee: 14 But I trust I shall shortly see thee, and we shall speak face to face. Peace be to thee. Our friends salute thee. Greet the friends by name.

John concludes the letter by stating there is more to be said. He writes that he will tell them in person rather than by letter. This may be due to the credibility attached to speaking in person rather than in writing. John uses the word "friends" twice. The Epicurean philosophers of the time also called each other "friends." John could be utilizing this terminology to emphasize the unity and harmony that he and the local churches shared in regards to the truth.

BIBLE APPLICATION

AIM: Students will learn the importance of showing hospitality to other believers as they study and live the commandment to love.

John the elder desires that his friends prosper. He writes a message of love and encouragement and expects that they treat others with the same kindness and compassion. Despite our good intentions or the results of our good works, the task of caring for others can still present risks. Whether we care for traveling evangelists, orphaned children, relatives, or even non-believers who ask for our help, there will always be challenges to our Christian compassion. Thankfully, as God presents us with opportunities to minister, He will open doors for us to include others who desire to help. We are not alone in our time of need or of sharing with others.

STUDENTS' RESPONSES

AIM: Students will commit to live their lives so that others can see they are walking in the truth of Christ.

We have all missed opportunities to show hospitality. Whether we overlooked someone's need or deliberately ignored a situation we could have easily assisted, we have all dropped the ball at some point. With John's message in mind, take time this week to show hospitality to strangers. Invite someone who is not like you to your home for a meal. At the end of the meal, offer to pray for them.

PRAYER

Jesus, You are kind, gracious, and caring. We learn from You how to show hospitality, kindness and care for those who struggle or need Your reassuring grace. Thank You and bless You. In Jesus' Name we pray. Amen.

DIG A LITTLE DEEPER

Throughout most of Christian history, traveling evangelists have depended upon the hospitality of the local congregations (as the apostle John and his contemporaries did in the First Century). Until fairly late in the Twentieth Century, Saints opened their homes to accommodate visiting preachers. But, over the last 40 years, it has become far more common for congregations and jurisdictions to secure hotel rooms as part of the remuneration for an invited guest speaker or revivalist. Though notwithstanding where the visiting preacher stays, the local congregations show hospitality when they pay the bill and provide meals and transportation.

God knows that hospitality is a blessing to the hospitable. He knows that something in us will only be satisfied as we share the things He has given us. He knows that we are designed to be conduits—He pours into us so that we can pour out to others. Beyond what we may do congregationally for our invited guests at church, we should seek out opportunities to be hospitable in our personal lives. We can host get-togethers for our friends, neighbors, and family. We can treat co-workers to lunch. We can throw someone a birthday party. Every believer is given the grace to be hospitable. We need only ask God for opportunities to express this grace.

HOW TO SAY IT

Malicious. ma-LIH-shus.

Preeminence. pre-EM-in-ins.

DAILY HOME BIBLE READINGS

MONDAY
All God's Works are Truth
(Daniel 4:34–37)

TUESDAY
Walk Before God in Faithfulness
(1 Kings 2:1–4)

WEDNESDAY
Truth is in Jesus
(Ephesians 4:17–25)

THURSDAY
Knowledge of the Truth
(Hebrews 10:23–27)

FRIDAY
Rightly Explain the Word of Truth
(2 Timothy 2:14–19)

SATURDAY
A Teacher in Faith and Truth
(1 Timothy 2:1–7)

SUNDAY
Coworkers with the Truth
(3 John)

PREPARE FOR NEXT SUNDAY

Read **1 Corinthians 12:1–11** and study "Gifts of the Spirit."

Sources:
Akin, Daniel, ed. *The New American Commentary.* Nashville, TN: Broadman and Holman. 2001.
Anders, Max and David Walls, eds. *Holman New Testament Commentary.* Nashville, TN: Broadman and Holman, 2000.
Keener, Craig S, ed. *IVP Bible Background Commentary.* Downers Grove, IL: InterVarsity Press, 1991.

GIFTS OF THE SPIRIT

BIBLE BASIS: 1 Corinthians 12:1–11

BIBLE TRUTH: One person does not possess all of the spiritual gifts; therefore, believers must work together for the church's common good.

MEMORY VERSE: "But the manifestation of the Spirit is given to every man to profit withal" (1 Corinthians 12:7).

LESSON AIM: By the end of the lesson, your students will: outline the purpose of spiritual gifts according to 1 Corinthians 12:1–11; appreciate individual spiritual gifts and the ways they are used; and uncover the spiritual gifts of the faith community and the ways they can be used for its benefit.

BIBLE BACKGROUND: 1 Corinthians 12:1–1; Romans 12:1–8—Read and incorporate the insights gained from the Background Scriptures into your study of the lesson.

LESSON SCRIPTURE

1 CORINTHIANS 12:1–11, KJV

1 Now concerning spiritual gifts, brethren, I would not have you ignorant.

2 Ye know that ye were Gentiles, carried away unto these dumb idols, even as ye were led.

3 Wherefore I give you to understand, that no man speaking by the Spirit of God calleth Jesus accursed: and that no man can say that Jesus is the Lord, but by the Holy Ghost.

4 Now there are diversities of gifts, but the same Spirit.

5 And there are differences of administrations, but the same Lord.

6 And there are diversities of operations, but it is the same God which worketh all in all.

7 But the manifestation of the Spirit is given to every man to profit withal.

8 For to one is given by the Spirit the word of wisdom; to another the word of knowl-edge by the same Spirit;

9 To another faith by the same Spirit; to another the gifts of healing by the same Spirit;

10 To another the working of miracles; to another prophecy; to another discerning of spirits; to another divers kinds of tongues; to another the interpretation of tongues:

11 But all these worketh that one and the selfsame Spirit, dividing to every man sev-erally as he will.

BIBLICAL DEFINITIONS

A. Administration (1 Cori thians 12:5) *diakonia* (Gk.)—service or office, ministering, especially those who execute the commands of others. **B. Operations (v. 6)** *energema* (Gk.)—activity, experience.

LIFE NEED FOR TODAY'S LESSON

AIM: Students will seek opportunities to become loyal contributing members of their societies.

INTRODUCTION
A Proper Perspective on Spiritual Gifts

The Corinthian church had been wrapped up in all kinds of immorality and unethical practices. Although it was a very gifted church in one of the most cosmopolitan cities in the Roman Empire, they were lacking in some basic Christian theology and behavior. In order to help them, Paul wrote the letter that we know as **1 Corinthians**. In **1 Corinthians**, we see Paul address a list of issues in the life of the church. This list of issues included celebrity worship of Christian ministers, sexual immorality, eating foods offered to idols, head covering for women, and the proper way to host communion. Next he addresses the spiritual gifts and specifically the gift of tongues. In order to introduce the topic, Paul teaches the Corinthians the proper perspective on spiritual gifts.

BIBLE LEARNING

AIM: Students will respond to the tendency of some in the church to boast in their spiritual sophistication and power.

I. THE TEST OF THE SPIRIT (1 Corinthians 12:1–3)

Paul starts off this chapter by stating that he does not want the Corinthians to be ignorant about spiritual gifts. His desire is that they would be mature in their knowledge about what spiritual gifts are and how they operate in the church. He then reminds them of their life as Gentiles. As Gentiles, they worshiped idols. Many of them probably participated in the worship of Aphrodite and Poseidon, two popular gods. Paul said they were led and guided to worship these mute idols. By a Jewish mindset, these idols were blind and could not speak in the same dynamic way as the God of Israel (**Habakkuk 2:18–20; Psalm 135:16**).

Spiritual Guidance (verses 1–3)

1 Now concerning spiritual gifts, brethren, I would not have you ignorant.

To be "ignorant" (Gk. agnoeo, **ag-no-EH-o**) means not only a lack of knowledge, but also a lack of understanding that leads to error or even sin through mistake. In this instance, to be ignorant is to be wrong. Often we sin because we do not know or understand correctly. Concerning spiritual matters, this can have grave consequences for the body of Christ. Most disunity, bigotry, and other errors in the body of Christ are committed by well-meaning, devoted Christians who are either ignorant of the truth or wrong, concerning spiritual or other things of God. This is especially true concerning "spiritual gifts" (Gk. pneumatikos, **puh-nehoo-mah-teek-OSE**).

2 Ye know that ye were Gentiles, carried away unto these dumb idols, even as ye were led.

Paul was not impressed by their enthusiastic worship and religious frenzy. Idol worshipers (which many of them were) could boast of the same religious excitement. Spirited worship services are not necessarily evidence of the Holy Spirit. There are many kinds of spirits related to pagan idols. The Holy Spirit is the Spirit of Christ. Only one's attitude toward Christ and consideration for those in the body can distinguish which spirit you worship. Some who worship are gifted in music, others with enticing speech, many with elegant liturgical dance, and still others lively praise while paying little attention to the doctrines being taught—whether they are of Christ or not.

3 Wherefore I give you to understand, that no man speaking by the Spirit of God calleth Jesus accursed: and that no man can say that Jesus is the Lord, but by the Holy Ghost.

Under persecution, distress, or religious frenzy, believers were often forced or led to curse the name of Jesus. "Accursed be Jesus" could not come from the lips of one under the influence of the Holy Spirit (the Spirit of Christ). On the other hand, "Jesus is Lord" (Gk. kurios, **KOO-ree-ose**) was the battle cry of Christians. Kurios was the same title that the Romans demanded everybody who came under their power ascribe to Caesar, saying "Caesar is Lord!" But kurios was also the title given to Yahweh by Jews, God-fearers, and Christians alike. To say "Jesus is Lord" was to commit to ultimate loyalty to Jesus. Thus, those who would not be ignorant or wrong about the Holy Spirit must examine their confession of faith.

QUESTION 1

What is the reason Paul says "no one can say Jesus is the Lord but by the Holy Ghost" (**1 Corinthians 12:3**)?

II. THE UNITY OF THE SPIRIT (vv. 4–7)

The argument is furthered with a discussion centered on the unity of the Spirit. God grants many different spiritual gifts, which operate and serve the body of Christ in different ways. Paul underscores the fact that they all have the same source and they are all working toward the same purpose under the same leadership.

One Spirit, Many Gifts (verses 4–7)

4 Now there are diversities of gifts, but the same Spirit.

There are "diversities" (Gk. *diairesis*, **dee-EYEreh-sis**) of allocations of gifts, but they are derived from the same Holy Spirit. Paul wants to make it plain that there can be unity in diversity. It is the Spirit's function to connect, not divide. These gifts are given not for individual glory, but to glorify or edify the body of Christ as a whole. If one does

not want to be ignorant or go wrong, one must understand the underlying unity of the operations of the Holy Spirit, remembering that these people once worshiped many gods according to their function (i.e., war gods, fertility gods, gods of the harvest). This was not so with the Spirit of Christ. With the Holy Spirit, there is unity in diversity.

5 And there are differences of administrations, but the same Lord.

There are a variety or "differences" (the same Greek word as "diversities" in **v. 4**) of "adminstrations" (Gk. *diakonia*, **dee-ah-kohNEE-ah**) rendered at the command of the same Lord. As each has a different gift given by the same Spirit, each performs a different service command by the same Lord and Master. Once again, Paul emphasizes unity in diversity because the church was in danger of being fractured by the very instruments of God that should have brought them together. Monotheism (belief in one God) was relatively new outside of the Jewish faith in this region of the world. Thus, among the Corinthian Church, who were largely not former Jews but instead former Greeks who worshiped many gods, it was necessary to emphasize oneness of the Lord and operations of the Holy Spirit.

6 And there are diversities of operations, but it is the same God which worketh all in all.

There is again the same diairesis of "operations" (Gk. *energema*, **en-ER-gay-mah**, energy, efficacy, actions, or activities), but it is the same God that is active in all that happens. The Corinthians were divided by those who brought them to Christ and baptized them (**1 Corinthians 3:5–9**). Paul faults their immaturity in the faith. Using the metaphor of building a house, he shows how God is the general contractor, and he, Apollos, Cephas (Peter), and others who brought them the Gospel and nurtured them were mere subcontractors in building the temple of God (**1 Corinthians 3:10–23**).

The same principle is at work in Paul's rhetorical argument that all gifts are mere tools put into their hands by God to build up the body of Christ. Each member is a part of God's construction crew.

7 But the manifestation of the Spirit is given to every man to profit withal.

The spiritual gifts are given by the Spirit to be used in service of the Lord. With power and efficacy made possible by God, they are the manifestation of the Spirit in the Christian community for the good of all. It is not a benefit to the individual, but the whole community. It is a benefit to the individual only insofar as it enhances one's value to the community. However, the manifestation of the Spirit is given to each expressly for the benefit of the whole community. The body of Christ is Paul's metaphor for the functioning Christian community.

QUESTION 2

How can spiritual gifts be used to defend the doctrine of the Trinity (**1 Corinthians 12:4–6**)?

III. THE GIFTS OF THE SPIRIT (vv. 8–11)

Paul then lists the gifts of the Spirit. These gifts come from the Holy Spirit as opposed to natural talents and endowments. He begins with the word of wisdom. Next is the word of knowledge. After this, Paul mentions the gift of faith. Next Paul lists supernatural healing. Then he goes on to mention the working of miracles. Prophecy is listed after this. Then Paul mentions discerning of spirits. Lastly he mentions the gifts of tongues and interpretation of tongues.

Diverse Spiritual Tools (verses 8–11)

8 For to one is given by the Spirit the word of wisdom; to another the word of knowledge by the same Spirit;

Paul begins to list the toolbox of gifts given by the Spirit to build the temple of God, the body of Christ. He painstakingly emphasizes to these newcomers in Christ (**1 Corinthians 3:2**), who saw their gifts as a source of personal pride, that spiritual unity is the foundation for these diverse spiritual tools that have been given as gifts.

The first gifts are the tools for the teaching ministry of the church. The word or utterance of "knowledge" (Gk. *gnosis*, **GNO-sis**) is to know what to do in any given situation, and "wisdom" (Gk. *sophia*, **soh-FEE-ah**) is the knowledge of the best things to do according to God's will. They both come from the same Spirit and are used to build up the church with knowledge of what Jesus Christ would do in any given situation (**John 14:26**), and wisdom to understand the will of God for their mission in the world (**2 Peter 3:9**). This is the wisdom and knowledge that did not come from academic achievement alone, but from communion with God and the study of His Word.

9 To another faith by the same Spirit; to another the gifts of healing by the same Spirit;

Paul names faith as a gift and tool. Everyone has a measure of faith, especially those who claim personal salvation, which comes by faith. Paul has in mind here an all-encompassing trust in God that can move mountains (**Matthew 17:20–21**), cause blind people to see (**Matthew 9:29**), and lame people to walk (**Mark 2:5–12**). It was the faith of former slaves in America that built institutions of higher learning and great churches while bearing the burden of racism and slavery. This kind of faith is a gift and a mighty tool.

The gifts of faith and healing are closely associated throughout the Gospels. The gifts of healing, along with faith and prayer, are important tools in building Christian fellowship because they demonstrate the unity of the mind, body, and spirit. Even more than that, the laying on of hands, anointing with oil, and mutual prayer build intimacy as they bring healing both individually and communally.

10 To another the working of miracles; to another prophecy; to another discerning of spirits; to another divers kinds of tongues; to another the interpretation of tongues:

The Greek word for "miracles" is *dunamis* (**DOO-nah-mis**), or power. Miracles were a demonstration of power as evidenced by the Messianic age. When John sent his disciple to inquire whether Jesus was the Messiah or not, Jesus responded with a recitation of His demonstrations of power as evidence (**Matthew 11:2–5**).

The gift of prophecy is the ability to reveal the will of God for our lives and communities. The prophet through the Spirit knows the mind of God and speaks it into the lives of His people. The Spirit works either to rebuke those people or institutions who are not in the will of God by foretelling the dire consequences of their actions, or by advising people or institutions who seek God's guidance to live according to His will.

The discerning of spirits is the ability to distinguish whether one's performance of miracles is by the Holy Spirit or some other spirit. It is necessary to understand the source of a demonstration or power to know its intent.

Diverse kinds of "tongues" (Gk. *glossa*, **GLOHsah**) were not exactly the same as the Pentecost experience (**Acts 2:4**), where the Spirit enabled them to speak known foreign languages. In Corinth, they spoke unlearned languages that no one understood, except perhaps the one speaking or someone who had the gift of interpreting unknown tongues.

11 But all these worketh that one and the selfsame Spirit, dividing to every man severally as he will.

Again Paul reminds us that all the diversity of gifts has one source: the Spirit of God, who chooses who gets what gift. Therefore, no one has reason to boast. More importantly, one does not choose a gift; the Spirit chooses the person for the gift. The same Spirit that gives the gift, gives according to the will of God.

BIBLE APPLICATION

AIM: Students will put the common good of the church above their personal interests.

Those who are gifted often use their talents for their own profit and success. We can see this in the lives of famous entertainers and politicians. The gifts that God has given them are used to glorify themselves and afford extravagant, luxurious lifestyles. This way of thinking has infiltrated the church, and many have sought to use their spiritual gifts to amass wealth and fame. Paul lets us know this is not what the gifts are for. They are for building up the church and serving others. The spiritual gifts are not ours. We are called to steward what the Holy Spirit has given us for the good of others.

STUDENTS' RESPONSES

AIM: Students will distinguish between spiritual gifts and natural abilities or talents.

Our spiritual gifts are learned in community and experience. If you are not involved in a ministry of your church, then volunteer for a limited time to serve in a ministry you have been interested in. It could be the children's ministry, hospitality, or outreach to the community. After serving for a while, ask for feedback from the leader of the ministry and others who you have served with about what spiritual gift they may see in you. Be sure to let others know what spiritual gifts you see in them and encourage them as well.

PRAYER

Gracious God, You continue to bless in so many ways. We want to serve You as we serve others through the gifts and talents that You have given us. Thank You for allowing us to care for others as You continue to care for us. In Jesus' Name we pray. Amen.

DIG A LITTLE DEEPER

The doctrine of spiritual gifts—as it is taught in the modern church—reflects interests and teachings that have been seemingly ignored for centuries. The Pentecostal movement is barely 100 years old, birthed in the early Twentieth Century through the Azusa Street Revival (1906–1915). Moreover, it was some sixty more years until pneumatology began to be routinely taught in denominational and evangelical churches. The 1970s was the decade of rediscovered focus on the proper use and practice of spiritual gifts by the Body of Christ.

Students of church history and ecclesiology, in particular, began to seriously consider how the spiritual gifts empower personal ministry. This led to concerted efforts to identify and categorize the service, speaking, and sign gifts that operate in the Body. And one of the most influential works of research into this topic was Your Spiritual Gifts Can Help Your Church Grow (first published in 1979), by C. Peter Wagner. When Wagner began his academic investigation into the rapid growth of Pentecostalism in Central America, he was a fundamentalist and cessationist. The evidence he found convinced him that the spiritual gifts were alive and well in the Latin American Church and that rediscovering those gifts would energize church growth in North America as well. His seminal book, reprinted many times since, is a great resource for learning more about the revival of the doctrine of spiritual gifts in the modern church.

Ref.: Wagner, C. Peter. Your Spiritual Gifts Can Help Your Church Grow. Bloomington, MN: Chosen Books, 2012.

HOW TO SAY IT

Discerning.	dih-**SER**-ning.
Diversities.	di-**VER**-si-tees.

DAILY HOME BIBLE READINGS

MONDAY
Not Exalted Over Other Members
(Deuteronomy 17:14–20)

TUESDAY
God's Gifts and Calling are
Irrevocable (Romans 11:25–32)

WEDNESDAY
God Distributed Gifts of the Spirit
(Hebrews 2:1–9)

THURSDAY
Grace Gifts Given to Us
(Romans 12:1–8)

FRIDAY
Understanding the Gifts God
Bestows (1 Corinthians 2:11–16)

SATURDAY
Gifts That Build Up the Church
(1 Corinthians 14:1–5)

SUNDAY
One Spirit, a Variety of Gifts
(1 Corinthians 12:1–11)

PREPARE FOR NEXT SUNDAY
Read **1 Corinthians 12:14–31** and study
"The Spirit Creates One Body."

Sources:
Hays, Richard B. *First Corinthians: Interpretation, A Bible Commentary for Teaching and Preaching.* Louisville, KY: John Knox. 1997.
Henry, Matthew. *Matthew Henry's Commentary on the Whole Bible: Complete and Unabridged in One Volume.* Peabody, MA: Hendrickson, 1994.
Utley, Robert James. *Paul's Letters to a Troubled Church: I and II Corinthians.* Study Guide Commentary Series, vol. 6. Marshall, TX: Bible Lessons International, 2002.

COMMENTS / NOTES:

THE SPIRIT CREATES ONE BODY

BIBLE BASIS: 1 Corinthians 12:14–31

BIBLE TRUTH: The church needs all the spiritual gifts to work together to function effectively and efficiently.

MEMORY VERSE: "For by one Spirit are we all baptized into one body, whether we be Jews or Gentiles, whether we be bond or free; and have been all made to drink into one Spirit" (1 Corinthians 12:13).

LESSON AIM: By the end of the lesson, your students will: learn how each member of the body supports the other members; value the different gifts operating within the church; and use spiritual gifts in cooperation with others for building up the body of Christ.

BIBLE BACKGROUND: 1 Corinthians 12:12–31; Galatians 3:23–29—Read and incorporate the insights gained from the Background Scriptures into your study of the lesson.

LESSON SCRIPTURE

1 CORINTHIANS 12:14–31, KJV

14 For the body is not one member, but many.

15 If the foot shall say, Because I am not the hand, I am not of the body; is it therefore not of the body?

16 And if the ear shall say, Because I am not the eye, I am not of the body; is it therefore not of the body?

17 If the whole body were an eye, where were the hearing? If the whole were hear-ing, where were the smelling?

18 But now hath God set the members every one of them in the body, as it hath pleased him.

19 And if they were all one member, where were the body?

20 But now are they many members, yet but one body.

21 And the eye cannot say unto the hand, I have no need of thee: nor again the head to the feet, I have no need of you.

22 Nay, much more those members of the body, which seem to be more feeble, are necessary:

23 And those members of the body, which we think to be less honourable, upon these we bestow more abundant honour; and our uncomely parts have more abundant comeliness.

24 For our comely parts have no need: but God hath tempered the body together, having given more abundant honour to that part which lacked.

25 That there should be no schism in the body; but that the members should have the same care one for another.

26 And whether one member suffer, all the members suffer with it; or one member be honoured, all the members rejoice with it.

27 Now ye are the body of Christ, and members in particular.

28 And God hath set some in the church, first apostles, secondarily prophets, thirdly teachers, after that miracles, then gifts of healings, helps, governments, diversities of tongues.

29 Are all apostles? are all prophets? are all teachers? are all workers of miracles?

30 Have all the gifts of healing? do all speak with tongues? do all interpret?

31 But covet earnestly the best gifts: and yet shew I unto you a more excellent way.

BIBLICAL DEFINITIONS
A. Tempered (1 Corinthians 12:24) *sugkerannumi* (Gk.)—Mixed together, commingled, united one thing to another.
B. Schism (v. 25) *schisma* (Gk.)—A rent, division, or dissension.

LIFE NEED FOR TODAY'S LESSON

AIM: **Students will understand the importance for Christians to operate in unity within their spiritual gifts.**

INTRODUCTION
A Common Source for a Common Goal
Paul likens the church to a human body. He emphasizes that every member has an important function just like the parts of the body. Each and every member contributes to the health and functioning of the whole body. This makes every believer a necessary part of the body of Christ. He reminds them that God is the provider of all gifts, and that the Holy Spirit is the source (**1 Corinthians 12:2–5**). As a balance, he illustrates the similarity of the human body to the body of Christ (**1 Corinthians 12:13**). By breaking down the importance of each member, he makes it clear that the church's body cannot afford to be divided for any reason, whether from outside influence or internal disagreement. Even as the various parts serve differing functions, they have a common source and a common goal and cannot operate separate from one another.

BIBLE LEARNING
AIM: **Students will trust that love governs the exercise of all the gifts of the Spirit.**

I. THE PURPOSE OF THE PARTS (1 Corinthians 12:14–20)
Paul begins his analogy of the body of Christ by using very common language regarding the human body. He blends humor and a hint of irony to describe the rather silly way that people can treat each other. Paul uses rhetorical questions to state the fact that the church is one body. If the church is made up of only one member or one spiritual gift, then it would miss out on some important things that it needed. In contrast, God has placed all of the members of the church into one body; thus the diversity of gifts can profit the whole church.

Strength in Diversity (verses 14–20)
14 For the body is not one member, but many.

The body metaphor was widely used in the ancient world. Many politicians used it to create peace and harmony between the different social classes. The argument was usually that the lower parts needed to be subordinated under the more superior or noble parts. In other words, the poor and working classes must submit to the rich and noble classes. This was not the case with Paul. The metaphor of the body is used in a more egalitarian way for Paul to show what true Christian community looks like. It can be safe to infer that for Paul, the idea of the church as the body of Christ was more than a metaphor but an actual reality.

Here Paul uses the body metaphor to highlight the necessity of diversity. Everyone cannot have the same gift if the body of Christ is to operate effectively. The body must consist of many members with diverse gifts. The oneness of the body does not take away from the diversity of its members.

15 If the foot shall say, Because I am not the hand, I am not of the body; is it therefore not of the body? 16 And if the ear shall say, Because I am not the eye, I am not of the body; is it therefore not of the body?

In many cultures, the foot is regarded as being very lowly. To touch another person with the foot would be considered disrespectful, if not insulting. But the touching of hands is considered a gesture of friendship. Thus, if the foot did not wish to belong to the body, because it did not have the status of a hand, that would not change that it is still a vital part of the body in reality.

The ear and the eye both occupy a position upon the head, so there is not as great a difference in status as the foot and the hand. However, the difference lies in function. These two organs have distinct purposes, neither of which the body would gladly do without.

17 If the whole body were an eye, where were the hearing? If the whole were hearing, where were the smelling?

The argument for diversity continues. The body of Christ cannot function properly with prophecy only, but also healing, hospitality, teaching, etc. Paul's point is that if the whole consisted of only one thing, the body would lose many functions, if not its very existence. The body was not meant to just pursue one function. Paul argues that a diversity of gifts are needed for the church to do all the work it is meant to do.

18 But now hath God set the members every one of them in the body, as it hath pleased him. 19 And if they were all one member, where were the body? 20 But now are they many members, yet but one body.

Paul credits God with having arranged each member of the body by plan. The body is organized for God's purpose. There would not be a body if He had not planned it, if all the members were the same. Diversity is necessary. According to God's purpose, many diverse members work together for the good of the whole body.

QUESTION 1

What is the reason that God set the members in one body (**1 Corinthians 12:18**)?

II. THE DANGER OF DIVISION (vv. 21–26)

Paul continues his conversation among the body parts by shedding light on very common attitudes. He supposes the eye and hand suffer a disagreement in which they attempt to cast each other off (**v. 21**). While it is quite possible for a body to survive an amputation of an eye or hand (or foot or arm, etc.), the point is that a seeing eye still has nothing with which to grasp. Likewise, a hand without an eye to guide it will do more bumbling and destruction rather than productive handiwork. Far too often, arguments rise in the church wherein members work harder to find fault in each other than they do to find alternate solutions to a common problem. More serious is the idea of "schism" (Gk. *schisma*, **SKHIZ-mah**). This word describes a division or dissention. More seriously, it represents a tear or a rip, as in a garment. Whenever we look upon our brothers and sisters as being less valuable—either to God or mankind—we are forgetting our own personal need for salvation.

The Body of Christ as One (verses 21–26)

21 And the eye cannot say unto the hand, I have no need of thee: nor again the head to the feet, I have no need of you.

One member or body part does not equal a body. Paul ties the existence of the body to the diversity of its members such that the Corinthian church could not protest his argument for diversity and interdependence. The many members make up the one body. Since the existence of the body is wrapped up in its diversity, then interdependence becomes necessary. None of the parts can exist alone; they all need each other to function as one body.

22 Nay, much more those members of the body, which seem to be more feeble, are necessary: 23 And those members of the body, which we think to be less honourable, upon these we bestow more abundant honour; and our uncomely parts have more abundant comeliness.

Here Paul overturns the Corinthians' attitude of pride and boasting. The parts of the body that seem weakest and least important are the most necessary. The parts with less honor and dignity are also the ones given the most care. Those that are weakest are those we clothe with the greatest care.

The parts that are stronger do not receive the same kind of care and attention.

For the Corinthian church, this means that those members they deem less dignified and lacking in knowledge are the ones to be treated with honor. The ones they despised for being weaker and an embarrassment were actually placed there by God to receive greater honor and care. This profound statement was rooted in the design of the body and therefore a part of God's plan.

24 For our comely parts have no need: but God hath tempered the body together, having given more abundant honour to that part which lacked. 25 That there should be no schism in the body; but that the members should have the same care one for another.

Continuing with the theme of interdependence and unity, Paul says that God has mixed the body together and given more honor to the parts that naturally lack it so that there would not be a schism in the body. The opposite of division is that the different members would provide the same care for one another. There would be no member who was isolated and did not receive the same care as the others. That would be detrimental for the health of the body and contrary to their existence as the body of Christ.

26 And whether one member suffer, all the members suffer with it; or one member be honoured, all the members rejoice with it.

With our physical bodies, an injury to any part is felt throughout the body. So it is with the body of Christ. Similarly, if one member exercises his or her gifts for the glory of the Lord, the whole of the church is edified. We see this edification in how the presence of a single member in a church can make an enormous difference in the quality of worship, in the feeling of hospitality visitors receive, even in the effectiveness of the church's administrative functions.

QUESTION 2

What is the reason Paul gives for honoring less honorable members in the body of Christ (**vv. 24–25**)?

III. THE MISSION OF MEMBERSHIP (vv. 27–31)

As Paul concludes this portion of his letter, he calls the discorporated body parts into a unified vision of hope. He addresses them directly, saying, "Now ye are the body of Christ and members in particular" (v. 27). As such he outlines that rather than lowly feet or eye or hand, the members of the church are actually far more vital. Naming gifts like prophecy, teaching, healing, preaching, and administration, he makes it clear that there is no person or gift that is without value in God's eyes (vv. 27–31).

Connected as One Body (verses 27–31)

27 Now ye are the body of Christ, and members in particular.

Paul underlines what he has been teaching throughout this passage. The members of the Corinthian church were the body of Christ. As individuals, they were members or parts of that body. Their existence as the body of Christ is based on their unity and interdependence. It was not an either/or proposition, but a both/ and proposition.

28 And God hath set some in the church, first apostles, secondarily prophets, thirdly teachers, after that miracles, then gifts of healings, helps, governments, diversities of tongues. 29 Are all apostles? are all prophets? are all teachers? are all workers of miracles? 30 Have all the gifts of healing? do all speak with tongues? do all interpret?

Now Paul goes back to the beginning of his argument in **1 Corinthians 12:12**. There are many members but one body. He states that God has set some in the church with different gifts. Four gifts are mentioned here that are not mentioned in the beginning of the chapter: apostles, prophets, teachers, and governments. All four are stated as roles or leadership positions with the final one potentially encompassing a number of types of leadership including administration. Paul includes them all here as spiritual gifts.

To be an apostle (Gk. *apostolos*, **ah-PO-stel-ose**) is literally to be "one who is sent." This applies to the twelve apostles who traveled with Jesus during His earthly ministry, as well as others, including Paul, who came after Jesus who have been specially commissioned by Him to be His witness and lay the foundation for the church. The other three gifts Paul mentions here have similarly important roles in spreading the Gospel. The prophet is one who hears from and speaks for God. Teachers regularly educate the members of the emerging church. "Governments" can be defined as the gift of administration or organizing.

He next asks some rhetorical questions. All of them can be answered with an emphatic "No!" The main point he is making is that not everyone can be every gift. He is continuing his argument for the diversity of gifts within the church. Everyone should not have the same gifts, or the church would cease to be a functioning body. This is the practical application of Paul's earlier statements about the whole body being an ear or an eye; there would be a loss of function. Paul is now making it plain that we do not all have, and should not all seek to have, the same gifts.

31 But covet earnestly the best gifts: and yet shew I unto you a more excellent way.

The word for covet earnestly (Gk. *zeloo*, **zeh-LOoh**) means to burn with zeal. Here Paul says to seek after the best gifts with intense passion. We can see that Paul wants to encourage spiritual gifts actively functioning in the church. He says to covet earnestly the best gifts. From this text, we cannot see what the best gifts are. It could be a way to appeal to the Corinthians' fascination with the more ecstatic supernatural gifts, or linked to his preference of prophecy as the best gift (cf. **1 Corinthians 14:1**).

Paul adds a qualifier to his encouragement to seek out the best gifts. He says that he will show them a more excellent (Gk. *hyperbole*, **hoo-pairbow-LAY**) way. Literally, this Greek word means "throwing beyond." Metaphorically it is an adjective describing something beyond measure. Paul is now about to show them a way that is beyond all measure of goodness. This is a transition into Paul's famous passage about love. It is clear from this transition that Paul's chapter on the qualities and the importance of love are set in the context of the spiritual gifts and his teaching on the diversity and unity of the body of Christ.

BIBLE APPLICATION

AIM: Students will recognize and support all parts of the body of Christ.

Often people separate from a church after a negative experience. Sometimes people can be put off by a well-intentioned but poorly placed comment. The news is unfortunately replete with accounts of people suffering tragic abuse at the hands of church leaders. Our natural reaction may be to say how much better we are than a particular denomination. We may go so far as to speak negatively about that particular group's theology based on human failures. Our task in striving for unity is not to condone or cover misdeeds done in or around the church. Instead, we should hold each other up via upholding standards and accountability. While it is hard to subject ourselves to each other, it is best that we determine that we will submit together to the will of God.

STUDENTS' RESPONSES

AIM: Students will strive to identify and understand their gifts and how they can best be used for the glory of God.

In some church cultures, the idea of spiritual gifts is only understood to be evident by certain worship activities. In the African American culture, it is no secret that exuberant singing, shouting, dancing, or displays of emotion may indeed reflect the power of the Holy Spirit upon someone's life and physical body. Still, Paul's letter makes certain that our gifts are not simply to be seen or heard within the assembly. Seek out those people in your church body who contribute behind the scenes. Make a point to show them appreciation through words of encouragement, a card, or a gift.

PRAYER

Praises and honor to the Creator of all gifts. We are excited and rejoice at knowing that each of us has a gift from God to glorify Jesus, our true Savior. In Jesus' Name we pray. Amen.

DIG A LITTLE DEEPER

The portrait of the church as the "body of Christ" is brimming with symbolism. Dr. Greg Lanier, associate professor of New Testament at Reformed Theological Seminary, has highlighted four major implications of the metaphor that we should recognize. Calling the Church "the body of Christ" emphasizes how each individual believer is spiritually united to Christ Himself. Of course, this is the direct statement we find in Ephesians 5:30. The same sentiment is expressed in 1 Corinthians 6:15, where we are reminded of our connectedness to the Lord as a part of an admonition to stay free of ungodly entanglements. The natural extension is another implication, that Christ is the head of the body. Mentioned explicitly in the prison epistles (Eph. 1:22,23; Col. 1:18), the headship of Christ is the mechanism by which the Church is nourished and cared for (Eph. 5:29; Col. 2:19).

The body metaphor also explains how individual Saints can constitute one entity—how there is diversity in the unity of the body. In one sense of the diversity in the Church, we liken the gifting and offices of members to how the physical body is composed of different organs (as we studied in this week's lesson text). But in another sense, diversity is represented by how the Church comprises different groups of people. In the early church, Jews and Gentiles were brought together to constitute one new people (Eph. 2:14–16; Eph. 3:6). The significance of this in our day is that the Church Universal is multi-racial and comprised of many ethnicities. Dr. Lanier's final implication is how believers are united to one another. This proceeds logically from the assertion that we are parts of the same body, but it is also explicitly mentioned in Romans 12:4,5 and Ephesians 4:25b. Holding these implications of the body metaphor in our thoughts will help us fully understand what it means to be a member of the Church. It would also be valuable to read Dr. Lanier's teaching on this topic in the June 2019 issue of Tabletalk magazine.

Ref.: Lanier, Greg. "Bodily Metaphors for the Christian Life." Tabletalk. June 2019.

HOW TO SAY IT

Schism.　　SKIH-zim.

Feeble.　　FEE-bul.

DAILY HOME BIBLE READINGS

MONDAY
Speaking with One Voice
(Exodus 19:1–8)

TUESDAY
We Will Be Obedient
(Exodus 24:1–7)

WEDNESDAY
Sincere and Pure Devotion
(2 Corinthians 11:1–5)

THURSDAY
Living in Harmony
(Romans 15:1–7)

FRIDAY
One Spirit, One Mind
(Philippians 1:21–30)

SATURDAY
One in Christ Jesus
(Galatians 3:23–29)

SUNDAY
Many Members, One Body
(1 Corinthians 12:14–31)

PREPARE FOR NEXT SUNDAY

Read **1 Corinthians 13** and study "The Greatest Gift is Love"

Sources:
Hays, Richard B. *First Corinthians: Interpretation, A Bible Commentary for Teaching and Preaching*. Louisville, KY: John Knox. 1997.
Henry, Matthew. *Matthew Henry's Commentary on the Whole Bible: Complete and Unabridged in One Volume*. Peabody, MA: Hendrickson, 1994.
Prime, Derek. *Opening Up 1 Corinthians*. Opening Up Commentary. Leominster, UK: Day One Publications, 2005.
Utley, Robert James. *Paul's Letters to a Troubled Church: I and II Corinthians*. Study Guide Commentary Series, vol. 6. Marshall, TX: Bible Lessons International, 2002.

THE GREATEST GIFT IS LOVE

BIBLE BASIS: 1 Corinthians 13

BIBLE TRUTH: Love is needed to fully achieve the benefit of all spiritual gifts.

MEMORY VERSE: "And now abideth faith, hope, charity, these three; but the greatest of these is charity" (1 Corinthians 13:13).

LESSON AIM: By the end of this lesson, your students will: explore the meaning of love as seen in 1 Corinthians 13; feel appreciation for one another in love; and seek a variety of ways to express love.

BIBLE BACKGROUND: 1 Corinthians 13; Ephesians 3:14–21—Read and incorporate the insights gained from the Background Scriptures into your study of the lesson.

LESSON SCRIPTURE

1 CORINTHIANS 13, KJV

1 Though I speak with the tongues of men and of angels, and have not charity, I am become as sounding brass, or a tinkling cymbal.

2 And though I have the gift of prophecy, and understand all mysteries, and all knowledge; and though I have all faith, so that I could remove mountains, and have not charity, I am nothing.

3 And though I bestow all my goods to feed the poor, and though I give my body to be burned, and have not charity, it prof-iteth me nothing.

4 Charity suffereth long, and is kind; char-ity envieth not; charity vaunteth not itself, is not puffed up,

5 Doth not behave itself unseemly, seeketh not her own, is not easily provoked, thinketh no evil;

6 Rejoiceth not in iniquity, but rejoiceth in the truth;

7 Beareth all things, believeth all things, hopeth all things, endureth all things.

8 Charity never faileth: but whether there be prophecies, they shall fail; whether there be tongues, they shall cease; whether there be knowledge, it shall vanish away.

9 For we know in part, and we prophesy in part.

10 But when that which is perfect is come, then that which is in part shall be done away.

11 When I was a child, I spake as a child, I understood as a child, I thought as a child: but when I became a man, I put away childish things.

12 For now we see through a glass, darkly; but then face to face: now I know in part; but then shall I know even as also I am known.

13 And now abideth faith, hope, charity, these three; but the greatest of these is charity.

BIBLICAL DEFINITIONS

A. Charity (1 Corinthians 13:1–4) *agape* (Gk.)—Love, fellowship, affection, benevolence, or specifically divine kindness.

B. Hope (v. 13) *elpis* (Gk.)—Expectation, confidence, or what is longed for.

LIFE NEED FOR TODAY'S LESSON

AIM: Students will accept that love is the primary requirement for societies attempting to make a dramatic influence on the world around them.

INTRODUCTION

The Divine Love

1 Corinthians 13 is often misinterpreted, which leads to improper application. This is not a mere ode to the virtues of love. Paul is using these words to address specific issues in the Corinthian church: selfishness, division, abuse of gifts, and envying of others' gifts.

The Greek term for love used in this chapter is *agape* (ah-GAH-pay). This word is closely associated with the Hebrew word *khesed* (KHESS-ed) which refers to God's covenant love for His people. Because of this association, agape became a key word for describing God's character and took on the meaning of a divine love that is deeply loyal. Believers should emulate this love, and Paul highlights its importance in this letter to the Corinthians.

BIBLE LEARNING

AIM: Students will affirm with Paul that love is the guarantee of the manifestations of the Spirit for the building up of the church.

I. LOVE IS SUPERIOR TO OTHER SPIRITUAL GIFTS (1 Corinthians 13:1–3)

Paul begins by demonstrating the superiority of love. The Corinthians held eloquence in especially high esteem and were somewhat preoccupied with the gift of tongues. However, even the most sophisticated gift of tongues, speaking the languages of men and angels, is just noise if not exercised in love.

The Necessity of Love (verses 1–3)

1 Though I speak with the tongues of men and of angels, and have not charity, I am become as sounding brass, or a tinkling cymbal.

The word "charity" here means love, heavenly love, affection, goodwill, or benevolence. Agape love means the decentering of the ego. The person is no longer the center of his or her universe or ultimate concern; "the other" is now in the center. Love is a radical reordering of priorities and ultimate values. Without love, everything we do is for our own self-glorification and benefit. With love, what we do is for God and others. Love is not a feeling; it is what we do for others without regard for self. It is partaking in the very nature of God, because He is love (**1 John 4:8**).

Spirit-inspired speech spoken in ecstasy, different languages, brilliant human rhetoric, or superhuman entities means nothing if it is not of God. Any intention whose source is not the God of love is in vain. If the Spirit of God animates the body, love holds it together. Tongues without love are only noise.

2 And though I have the gift of prophecy, and understand all mysteries, and all knowledge; and though I have all faith, so that I could remove mountains, and have not charity, I am nothing.

The gift of prophecy or preaching is mere entertainment or scolding and has no effect if the speaker is not motivated by love. The gift of intellectual accomplishment without love leads to contempt and snobbery. The gift of great faith that achieves or sacrifices much can lead to false pride. Without love, none of these gifts edifies the body of Christ or pleases God.

3 And though I bestow all my goods to feed the poor, and though I give my body to be burned, and have not charity, it profiteth me nothing.

Benevolence and even self-sacrifice done with ill intention or with the wrong spirit might as well not be done at all. To give out of obligation, self-promotion, or even contempt is worse than not giving at all. It does not build up the body of Christ. Likewise, to seek persecution or make sacrifice for selfish intentions may very well hurt one's cause more than it helps.

Paul has made it clear that agape love is more important than spiritual gifts. In this passage, he explains exactly what agape is. Love is that which connects us to God and one another. Like the blood that circulates through the body's veins carrying oxygen and nutrients from cell to cell, so love also brings us into a life-giving relationship to God and one another.

II. CHARACTERISTICS OF LOVE (vv. 4–7)

In the King James Version, *agape* is translated "charity." When we think of charity, we usually think of giving to others, an active expression of Christian love. This was not the limit of the meaning of "charity" in King James' time, however. Back then, "charity" was understood as it related to the similar word "cherish." To show charity to someone was to show that you cherished them. This includes, but also goes far beyond, giving alms, as Paul further explains.

Love is incompatible with ill will. It does not seek its own honor, profit, or pleasure. Instead, love focuses on the well-being of others. It is not quarrelsome or vindictive. Instead, love "thinketh no evil," meaning that it keeps no account of wrongs.

Love is Amazing (verses 4–7)

4 Charity suffereth long, and is kind; charity envieth not; charity vaunteth not itself, is not puffed up,

Love "suffereth long" (Gk. *makrothumeo*, **mahkro-thoo-MEH-oh**), or endures patiently the errors, weaknesses, and even meanness of people. Love makes us slow to anger or slow to repay hurt for hurt. It will suffer many things for the sake of the relationship. Love is kind (Gk. *chresteuomai*, **khray-STEH-oo-oh-meye**); it shows kindness whenever possible. Love does not "envieth" (Gk. *zeloo*, **zay-LAH-oh**); it does not earnestly covet another's good fortune. Love does not get angry at another's success. Love does not "vaunteth" (Gk. *perpereuomai*, **per-per-EHOO-oh-meye**), or brag, about oneself. It is not boastful or stuck up. Love does not have a swollen head and is not "puffed up" (Gk. *phusioo*, **foo-see-AH-oh**), snobbish, or arrogant. A loving person esteems others higher than themselves.

5 Doth not behave itself unseemly, seeketh not her own, is not easily provoked, thinketh no evil;

Love is never rude; it is full of grace and charm. It does not go around hurting others' feelings. It always uses tact and politeness whenever possible. Love never demands its rights, but seeks its responsibilities toward others. It is not self-centered or self-assertive. Love does not fly off the handle. It does not lose its temper. It is not easily exasperated at people. Love does not keep the books on the wrong done to it. Love does not keep score in order to repay wrong for wrong. It forgives the evil that people do to it. It does not carry a grudge.

6 Rejoiceth not in iniquity, but rejoiceth in the truth;

Love does not like to hear about the moral failures of others. It does not get pleasure out of the misfortune of others. There is a sick joy from witnessing or hearing gossip about the misdeeds of others. We often judge our own righteousness and well-being as measured by the failings of others. However, love is happy to hear the truth (or what is right), no matter how painful. Love rejoices when what is true, correct, and righteous wins the day regardless of how that may impact it directly.

7 Beareth all things, believeth all things, hopeth all things, endureth all things.

If God is love and He created all things good, then love also is the progenitor of all things good. Love is our participation in God's nature. Thus, love is the only foundation for Christian community and relationships. Love, like God, is eternal. It "beareth"(Gk. *stego*, **STEH-goh**) the errors and faults of others. Love does not expose one's weakness because it does not rejoice in the misfortune of others. Yet it does not excuse sin or wrongdoing, because it equally rejoices in truth. Instead, as Christ bore our sin on the Cross, we take on the weakness and faults of others as though they were our own.

Love believes the best, trusts in the object of its love, has confidence in him or her, and gives credit to the object of love that may not be selfevident except through the eyes of love. Love can bear all things because it believes all things with the special insight that only a loving relationship can bring. Love "hopeth" (Gk. *elpizo*, **el-PID-zo**) with joy, full confidence in eager expectation the salvation of the Lord to come. It bears all things because it believes with only the insight of God the maker, thus it can wait for the true nature of people to reveal itself.

Love trusts in the eventual reconciliation with God. It "endureth" (Gk. *hupomeno*, **hoo-poMEN-oh**) and continues to be present; it does not perish or depart in spite of errors, faults, or wrongs done.

QUESTION 1

What are some of the characteristics of love (**1 Corinthians 13:4–7**)?

III. LOVE ENDURES (vv. 8–13)

Love surpasses all the other spiritual gifts because they will pass away, but it endures forever. Prophecy, tongues, and knowledge are limited (**v. 9**). Further, a time will come when those gifts will not be necessary. They are given by the Spirit for the building and maturation of the church. We will not need such things in heaven, but will experience love there.

Love is Forever (verses 8–13)

8 Charity never faileth: but whether there be prophecies, they shall fail; whether there be tongues, they shall cease; whether there be knowledge, it shall vanish away.

Love is eternal; it never comes to an end. It is absolutely permanent. Whereas all the gifts in which the Corinthians pride themselves are transitory at best, love is transcendent. Love is—exists only in and for—relationship, yet is more than the sum of its parts; like life itself, it is always renewed, even in the age to come.

The gifts, on the other hand, have no such guarantee. They were given by the Spirit as instruments to be used in this age. Paul anticipates that these gifts will no longer be needed when the next age occurs, marked by the return of Christ and fulfillment of the reign of God. They will pass away with the old age. Love, on the other hand, is essential, not instrumental; it will never pass away. In contrast, when all prophecy has been fulfilled, tongues will no longer be necessary as a language; signs, missions, and knowledge will vanish because there will be no more mysteries.

9 For we know in part, and we prophesy in part.

Love like God, is complete. On the other hand, we are imperfect creatures who can only comprehend reality—both material and spiritual—in an incomplete manner. Therefore, we can only preach or prophesy in an imperfect and partial way. For Paul, the kingdom of God was near, but not yet. It was not fully revealed in this age, so our knowledge and prophecy of it could only be partial.

10 But when that which is perfect is come, then that which is in part shall be done away.

The "perfect" (Gk. *teleios*, **TEL-ay-os**) maturity or completeness will come with the end of this present, imperfect age and the beginning of the new, perfect age—namely the "eschaton" (Gk. *eschatos*, **ES-khah-toce**, last, uttermost). Paul describes the times the Corinthians lived in as transitory at best. Thus they should not make gods or idols out of the gifts they esteem so highly, because their gifts are both imperfect and temporary.

11 When I was a child, I spake as a child, I understood as a child, I thought as a child: but when I became a man, I put away childish things.

Paul uses the metaphor of the maturing spiritual human being who grows from childhood to adulthood. The spiritual gifts become mere toys or childish things in people who do not love. Paul, who had called the Corinthians "babes in Christ," chided them once again

to grow up and put away their toys, in this case, using their gifts for the wrong reasons (**1 Corinthians 3:1**).

12 For now we see through a glass, darkly; but then face to face: now I know in part; but then shall I know even as also I am known.

Mirrors were a primary industry in the city of Corinth. Mirrors made in Corinth were made of finely polished silver and bronze. The image was often concave and distorted, much like the amusement park house of mirrors. Thus we see only dimly through the distorted reflections of our own limited apprehensions. However, when Jesus returns and God makes His dwelling place among His people, we will see face to face (**Revelation 21:22–23**).

When we look through a mirror, we see only a reflection of ourselves and have only a knowledge that is filtered through our senses. However, when we come face-to-face with another, we see clearly, but are also seen. We not only come to know, but also are known by another.

13 And now abideth faith, hope, charity, these three; but the greatest of these is charity.

After everything that has been said, we come to the conclusion of the matter. Spirit gifts are transient, given to a particular community, for a particular purpose, and for the particular time. It is childish to esteem them too highly. However, by faith we are saved according to the grace of God. In hope, we wait upon the return of Jesus and the coming of the reign of God. All this is due to God's love for us. These are what remain when one matures in Christ.

Love has revealed itself completely in the revelation of Jesus Christ in His life, death, and resurrection. Thus we can love the Holy One. Jesus says, "This is my commandment, That ye love one another, as I have loved you. Greater love hath no man than this, that a man lay down his life for his friends" (**John 15:12–13**). Love is the greatest.

QUESTION 2

Why is love superior to the other spiritual gifts (**v. 8**)?

BIBLE APPLICATION

AIM: Students will experience love as the difference in living a faithful life of obedience to God.

The Holy Sprit is the source of all the spiritual gifts and He decides which gifts each person will have (**1 Corinthians 12:11**). The spiritual gifts are given to strengthen other believers (**1 Corinthians 12:7**), not to gain personal status and position.

The gifts themselves should not be our primary focus. Love is an essential element in the exercise of spiritual gifts. It is good to desire spiritual gifts (**1 Corinthians 14:1**). However, love is superior to every gift. Prophecy, knowledge, and the demonstration of great faith must all reflect a genuine love and affection for people.

Websites and bookstores abound with assessments to help people discover their spiritual gifts. While the understanding and use of spiritual gifts is important, we must always exercise them in love.

STUDENTS' RESPONSES

AIM: Students will develop spiritually in their ability to express and live in Christian love.

Spiritual gifts cannot be effective if not used in love. Grow in your relationship with Christ. Show His love to those around you. Demonstrate the love of God as you use your spiritual gifts to help others grow and mature.

PRAYER

In times like these Lord, we need to know Your powerful and wonderful love. Thank You for loving us as we grow in loving the church and others. In Jesus' Name we pray. Amen.

DIG A LITTLE DEEPER

There is an important piece of background reading for a lesson like this. We should consult "The Doctrines of the Church of God in Christ" to review the Church's teaching about the Baptism of the Holy Ghost. (The Doctrines are reprinted, for our convenience, at the back of both the annual and the quarterly commentaries of the Sunday School lessons.) To quote: "We believe the baptism of the Holy Ghost is an experience subsequent to conversion and sanctification and that tongue-speaking is the consequence of the baptism in the Holy Ghost with the manifestation of the fruit of the spirit" (emphasis mine). As our founder Bishop C.H. Mason taught, Scripture demonstrates that spirit baptism is evidenced by speaking in tongues (Acts 2:4; Acts 10:44–46; Acts 19:1–6). To quote again from the Doctrine, "When one receives a baptismal Holy Ghost experience, we believe one will speak with a tongue unknown to oneself according to the sovereign will of Christ." In that sense, the initial experience of tongue-speaking for a believer is a sign that the believer is now filled with the Spirit.

However, the clear teaching of Scripture is that there is also a spiritual gift of tongues, distributed to believers as the Holy Ghost sees fit. "Do all speak with tongues?" Paul asked, referring to the gift (1 Cor. 12:30). The answer is "no" because the gift of tongues is not given to every believer (just as the gifts of the working of miracles and healing are not given to everyone). As my late Church Mother once said, "every Saint will have spoken in tongues once, but some may never speak in tongues again."

HOW TO SAY IT

Vaunteth.   VON-teth.

Bestow.   bi-STOW.

Sources:
English Standard Version Study Bible. Wheaton, IL: Crossway, 2007.
Henry, Matthew. *Matthew Henry's Commentary on the Whole Bible: Complete and Unabridged in One Volume*. Peabody, MA: Hendrickson, 1994.
Prime, Derek. *Opening Up 1 Corinthians*. Opening Up Commentary. Leominster, UK: Day One Publications, 2005.
Utley, Robert James. *Paul's Letters to a Troubled Church: I and II Corinthians*. Study Guide Commentary Series, vol. 6. Marshall, TX: Bible Lessons International, 2002.
Walvoord, John F., and Roy B. Zuck. *The Bible Knowledge Commentary: An Exposition of the Scriptures*. Dallas Theological Seminary. Wheaton, IL: Victor Books, 1985.
Wiersbe, Warren W. *The Bible Exposition Commentary*. Wheaton, IL: Victor Books, 1996.

DAILY HOME BIBLE READINGS

MONDAY
Love and the Knowledge of God
(Hosea 6:1–6)

TUESDAY
Abounding in Steadfast Love
(Jonah 3:10–4:11)

WEDNESDAY
Guided by the Spirit
(Galatians 5:19–26)

THURSDAY
Increasing Love for One Another
(2 Thessalonians 1:1–5)

FRIDAY
Love and Steadfastness
(2 Thessalonians 3:1–5)

SATURDAY
Filled with the Fullness of God
(Ephesians 3:14–21)

SUNDAY
Love Never Ends
(1 Corinthians 13)

PREPARE FOR NEXT SUNDAY
Read **Acts 2:1-7; 1 Corinthians 14:13-19** and study "Gift of Languages."

COMMENTS / NOTES:

The Symbol of the Church Of God In Christ

The Symbol of the Church Of God In Christ is an outgrowth of the Presiding Bishop's Coat of Arms, which has become quite familiar to the Church. The design of the Official Seal of the Church was created in 1973 and adopted in the General Assembly in 1981 (July Session).

The obvious GARNERED WHEAT in the center of the seal represents all of the people of the Church Of God In Christ, Inc. The ROPE of wheat that holds the shaft together represents the Founding Father of the Church, Bishop Charles Harrison Mason, who, at the call of the Lord, banded us together as a Brotherhood of Churches in the First Pentecostal General Assembly of the Church, in 1907.

The date in the seal has a two-fold purpose: first, to tell us that Bishop Mason received the baptism of the Holy Ghost in March 1907 and, second, to tell us that it was because of this outpouring that Bishop Mason was compelled to call us together in February of 1907 to organize the Church Of God In Christ.

The RAIN in the background represents the Latter Rain, or the End-time Revivals, which brought about the emergence of our Church along with other Pentecostal Holiness Bodies in the same era. The rain also serves as a challenge to the Church to keep Christ in the center of our worship and service, so that He may continue to use the Church Of God In Christ as one of the vehicles of Pentecostal Revival before the return of the Lord.

This information was reprinted from the book *So You Want to KNOW YOUR CHURCH* by Alferd Z. Hall, Jr.

COGIC AFFIRMATION OF FAITH

We believe the Bible to be the inspired and only infallible written Word of God.

We believe that there is One God, eternally existent in three Persons: God the Father, God the Son, and God the Holy Spirit.

We believe in the Blessed Hope, which is the rapture of the Church of God, which is in Christ at His return.

We believe that the only means of being cleansed from sin is through repentance and faith in the precious Blood of Jesus Christ.

We believe that regeneration by the Holy Ghost is absolutely essential for personal salvation.

We believe that the redemptive work of Christ on the Cross provides healing for the human body in answer to believing in prayer.

We believe that the baptism in the Holy Ghost, according to Acts 2:4, is given to believers who ask for it.

We believe in the sanctifying power of the Holy Spirit, by whose indwelling the Christian is enabled to live a Holy and separated life in this present world. Amen.

The Doctrines of the Church Of God In Christ

THE BIBLE

We believe that the Bible is the Word of God and contains one harmonious and sufficiently complete system of doctrine. We believe in the full inspiration of the Word of God. We hold the Word of God to be the only authority in all matters and assert that no doctrine can be true or essential if it does not find a place in this Word.

THE FATHER

We believe in God, the Father Almighty, the Author and Creator of all things. The Old Testament reveals God in diverse manners, by manifesting His nature, character, and dominions. The Gospels in the New Testament give us knowledge of God the "Father" or "My Father," showing the relationship of God to Jesus as Father, or representing Him as the Father in the Godhead, and Jesus himself that Son (St. John 15:8, 14:20). Jesus also gives God the distinction of "Fatherhood" to all believers when He explains God in the light of "Your Father in Heaven" (St. Matthew 6:8).

THE SON

We believe that Jesus Christ is the Son of God, the second person in the Godhead of the Trinity or Triune Godhead. We believe that Jesus was and is eternal in His person and nature as the Son of God who was with God in the beginning of creation (St. John 1:1). We believe that Jesus Christ was born of a virgin called Mary according to the Scripture (St. Matthew 1:18), thus giving rise to our fundamental belief in the Virgin

Birth and to all of the miraculous events surrounding the phenomenon (St. Matthew 1:18–25). We believe that Jesus Christ became the "suffering servant" to man; this suffering servant came seeking to redeem man from sin and to reconcile him to God, his Father (Romans 5:10). We believe that Jesus Christ is standing now as mediator between God and man (I Timothy 2:5).

THE HOLY GHOST
We believe the Holy Ghost or Holy Spirit is the third person of the Trinity; proceeds from the Father and the Son; is of the same substance, equal to power and glory; and is together with the Father and the Son, to be believed in, obeyed, and worshiped. The Holy Ghost is a gift bestowed upon the believer for the purpose of equipping and empowering the believer, making him or her a more effective witness for service in the world. He teaches and guides one into all truth (John 16:13; Acts 1:8, 8:39).

THE BAPTISM OF THE HOLY GHOST
We believe that the Baptism of the Holy Ghost is an experience subsequent to conversion and sanctification and that tongue-speaking is the consequence of the baptism in the Holy Ghost with the manifestations of the fruit of the spirit (Galatians 5:22–23; Acts 10:46, 19:1–6). We believe that we are not baptized with the Holy Ghost in order to be saved (Acts 19:1–6; John 3:5). When one receives a baptismal Holy Ghost experience, we believe one will speak with a tongue unknown to oneself according to the sovereign will of Christ. To be filled with the Spirit means to be Spirit controlled as expressed by Paul in Ephesians 5:18,19. Since the charismatic demonstrations were necessary to help the early church to be successful in implementing the command of Christ, we, therefore, believe that a Holy Ghost experience is mandatory for all believers today.

MAN
We believe that humankind was created holy by God, composed of body, soul, and spirit. We believe that humankind, by nature, is sinful and unholy. Being born in sin, a person needs to be born again, sanctified and cleansed from all sins by the blood of Jesus. We believe that one is saved by confessing and forsaking one's sins, and believing on the Lord Jesus Christ, and that having become a child of God, by being born again and adopted into the family of God, one may, and should, claim the inheritance of the sons of God, namely the baptism of the Holy Ghost.

SIN
Sin, the Bible teaches, began in the angelic world (Ezekiel 28:11–19; Isaiah 14:12–20) and is transmitted into the blood of the human race through disobedience and deception motivated by unbelief (I Timothy 2:14). Adam's sin, committed by eating of the forbidden fruit from the tree of knowledge of good and evil, carried with it permanent pollution or depraved human nature to all his descendants. This is called "original sin." Sin can now be defined as a volitional transgression against God and a lack of conformity to the will of God. We, therefore, conclude that humankind by nature is sinful and has fallen from a glorious and righteous state from which we were created, and has become unrighteous and unholy. We therefore, must be restored to the state of holiness from which we have fallen by being born again (St. John 3:7).

SALVATION
Salvation deals with the application of the work of redemption to the sinner with restoration to divine favor and communion with God. This redemptive operation of the Holy Ghost upon sinners is brought about by repentance toward God and faith toward our Lord Jesus Christ which brings conversion, faith, justification, regeneration, sanctification, and the baptism of the Holy Ghost. Repentance is the work of God, which results in a change of mind in respect to a person's relationship to God (St. Matthew 3:1–2, 4:17; Acts 20:21). Faith is a certain conviction wrought in the heart by the Holy Spirit, as to the truth of the Gospel and a heart trust in the promises of God in Christ (Romans 1:17, 3:28; St. Matthew 9:22; Acts 26:18). Conversion is that act of God whereby He causes the regenerated sinner, in one's conscious life, to turn to Him in repentance and faith (II Kings 5:15; II Chronicles 33:12,13; St. Luke 19:8,9; Acts 8:30). Regeneration is the act of God by which the principle of the new life is implanted in humankind, the governing disposition of soul is made holy, and the first holy exercise of this new disposition is secured. Sanctification is that gracious and continuous operation of the Holy Ghost, by which He delivers the justified sinner from the pollution of sin, renews a person's whole nature in the image of God, and enables one to perform good works (Romans 6:4, 5:6; Colossians 2:12, 3:1).

ANGELS
The Bible uses the term "angel" (a heavenly body) clearly and primarily to denote messengers or ambassadors of God with such Scripture references as Revelations 4:5, which indicates their duty in heaven to praise God (Psalm 103:20), to do God's will (St. Matthew 18:10), and to behold His face. But since heaven must come down to earth, they also have a mission to earth. The Bible indicates that they accompanied God in the Creation, and also that they will accompany Christ in His return in Glory.

DEMONS
Demons denote unclean or evil spirits; they are sometimes called devils or demonic beings. They are evil spirits, belonging to the unseen or spiritual realm, embodied in human beings. The Old Testament refers to the prince of demons, sometimes called Satan (adversary) or Devil, as having power and wisdom, taking the habitation of other forms such as the serpent (Genesis 3:1). The New Testament speaks of the Devil as Tempter (St. Matthew 4:3), and it goes on to tell the works of

Satan, the Devil, and demons as combating righteousness and good in any form, proving to be an adversary to the saints. Their chief power is exercised to destroy the mission of Jesus Christ. It can well be said that the Christian Church believes in demons, Satan, and devils. We believe in their power and purpose. We believe they can be subdued and conquered as in the commandment to the believer by Jesus. "In my name they shall cast out Satan and the work of the Devil and to resist him and then he will flee (WITHDRAW) from you" (St. Mark 16:17).

THE CHURCH

The Church forms a spiritual unity of which Christ is the divine head. It is animated by one Spirit, the Spirit of Christ. It professes one faith, shares one hope, and serves one King. It is the citadel of the truth and God's agency for communicating to believers all spiritual blessings. The Church then is the object of our faith rather than of knowledge. The name of our Church, "CHURCH OF GOD IN CHRIST," is supported by I Thessalonians 2:14 and other passages in the Pauline Epistles. The word "CHURCH" or "EKKLESIA" was first applied to the Christian society by Jesus Christ in St. Matthew 16:18, the occasion being that of His benediction of Peter at Caesarea Philippi.

THE SECOND COMING OF CHRIST

We believe in the second coming of Christ; that He shall come from heaven to earth, personally, bodily, visibly (Acts 1:11; Titus 2:11–13; St. Matthew 16:27, 24:30, 25:30; Luke 21:27; John 1:14, 17; Titus 2:11); and that the Church, the bride, will be caught up to meet Him in the air (I Thessalonians 4:16–17). We admonish all who have this hope to purify themselves as He is pure.

DIVINE HEALING

The Church Of God In Christ believes in and practices Divine Healing. It is a commandment of Jesus to the Apostles (St. Mark 16:18). Jesus affirms His teachings on healing by explaining to His disciples, who were to be Apostles, that healing the afflicted is by faith (St. Luke 9:40–41). Therefore, we believe that healing by faith in God has scriptural support and ordained authority. St. James's writings in his epistle encourage Elders to pray for the sick, lay hands upon them and to anoint them with oil, and state that prayers with faith shall heal the sick and the Lord shall raise them up. Healing is still practiced widely and frequently in the Church Of God In Christ, and testimonies of healing in our Church testify to this fact.

MIRACLES

The Church Of God In Christ believes that miracles occur to convince people that the Bible is God's Word. A miracle can be defined as an extraordinary visible act of divine power, wrought by the efficient agency of the will of God, which has as its final cause the vindication of the righteousness of God's Word. We believe that the works of God, which were performed during the beginnings of Christianity, do and will occur even today where God is preached, faith in Christ is exercised, the Holy Ghost is active, and the Gospel is promulgated in the truth (Acts 5:15, 6:8, 9:40; Luke 4:36, 7:14, 15, 5:5, 6; St. Mark 14:15).

THE ORDINANCES OF THE CHURCH

It is generally admitted that for an ordinance to be valid, it must have been instituted by Christ. When we speak of ordinances of the church, we are speaking of those instituted by Christ, in which by sensible signs the grace of God in Christ and the benefits of the covenant of grace are represented, sealed, and applied to believers, and these in turn give expression to their faith and allegiance to God. The Church Of God In Christ recognizes three ordinances as having been instituted by Christ himself and, therefore, are binding upon the church practice.

THE LORD'S SUPPER (HOLY COMMUNION)

The Lord's Supper symbolizes the Lord's death and suffering for the benefit and in the place of His people. It also symbolizes the believer's participation in the crucified Christ. It represents not only the death of Christ as the object of faith, which unites the believers to Christ, but also the effect of this act as the giving of life, strength, and joy to the soul. The communicant by faith enters into a special spiritual union of one's soul with the glorified Christ.

FOOT WASHING

Foot washing is practiced and recognized as an ordinance in our Church because Christ, by His example, showed that humility characterized greatness in the kingdom of God, and that service rendered to others gave evidence that humility, motivated by love, exists. These services are held subsequent to the Lord's Supper; however, its regularity is left to the discretion of the pastor in charge.

WATER BAPTISM

We believe that Water Baptism is necessary as instructed by Christ in St. John 3:5, "UNLESS MAN BE BORN AGAIN OF WATER AND OF THE SPIRIT..."

However, we do not believe that water baptism alone is a means of salvation, but is an outward demonstration that one has already had a conversion experience and has accepted Christ as his personal Savior. As Pentecostals, we practice immersion in preference to sprinkling because immersion corresponds more closely to the death, burial, and resurrection of our Lord (Colossians 2:12). It also symbolizes regeneration and purification more than any other mode. Therefore, we practice immersion as our mode of baptism. We believe that we should use the Baptismal Formula given to us by Christ for all "...IN THE NAME OF THE FATHER, AND OF THE SON, AND OF THE HOLY GHOST..." (Matthew 28:19).

Suggested Order of Service

1. Call to order.

2. Singing.

3. Prayer.

4.

New Responsive Reading & Core Values

ISSD: Responsive Reading

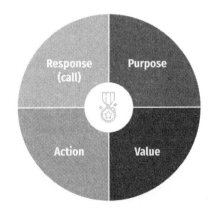

Calls for the response of worship of God
Calls for response to God (in unity)
Calls for response to God's truth

Builds identity around our core values
Builds student belief in themselves and in the mission of The Church

- To support students in achieving the curricular outcomes
- To inspire students to become engaged in comprehension and practice of scriptural commands

- For the life of The Church, it is:
  - -biblical
  - -historic
  - -participatory
  - -instructional

Suggested Order of Service

Responsive reading continued:

Sunday School's Core Values

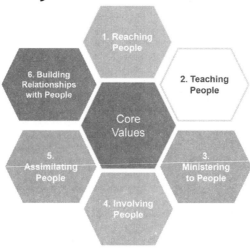

Core Values in Detail

01	02	03	04	05	06
Reaching People	**Teaching People**	**Ministering to People**	**Involving People**	**Assimilating People**	**Building Relationships**
We believe that Sunday School should have a two-fold focus: sharing the gospel and teaching biblical principles for life application.	We believe that recruiting and developing leaders is top priority.	We believe that this can be accomplished by creating care groups within the Sunday School.	We believe that Sunday School should equip and give every member an opportunity to serve Christ.	We teach that getting visitors and new members involved in Sunday School is the best way to keep them in the Church.	We believe that relationships are one of the main reasons why people attend Sunday School.

SUPERINTENDENT/TEACHER: Behold how good and how pleasant it is for brethren to dwell together in unity! *Psalm 133:1*

SCHOOL/CLASS: But to do good and to communicate forget not: for with such sacrifices God is well pleased. *Hebrews 13:16*

SUPERINTENDENT/TEACHER: All scripture is given by inspiration of God, and is profitable for doctrine, for reproof, for correction, for instruction in righteousness. *2 Timothy 3:16*

SCHOOL/CLASS: Thy word is a lamp unto my feet, and a light unto my path. *Psalm 119:105*

SUPERINTENDENT/TEACHER: Look not every man on his own things, but every man also on the things of others. *Philippians 2:4*

SCHOOL/CLASS: He that hath a bountiful eye shall be blessed; for he giveth of his bread to the poor. *Proverbs 22:9*

SUPERINTENDENT/TEACHER: Wherefore he saith, When he ascended up on high, he led captivity captive, and gave gifts unto men. *Ephesians 4:8*

SCHOOL/CLASS: As every man hath received the gift, even so minister the same one to another, as good stewards of the manifold grace of God. *1 Peter 4:10*

SUPERINTENDENT/TEACHER: For as the body is one, and hath many members, and all the members of that one body, being many, are one body: so also is Christ. *1 Corinthians 12:12*

SCHOOL/CLASS: For as we have many members in one body, and all members have not the same office. *Romans 12:4*

SUPERINTENDENT/TEACHER: By this shall all men know that ye are my disciples, if ye have love one to another. *John 13:35*

SCHOOL/CLASS: For, brethren, ye have been called unto liberty; only use not liberty for an occasion to the flesh, but by love serve one another. *Galatians 5:13*

SUPERINTENDENT/ALL: But grow in grace, and in the knowledge of our Lord and Saviour Jesus Christ. To him be glory both now and for ever. Amen. *2 Peter 3:18*

Notes

Notes

Notes

Notes

Notes

Notes

Notes

Notes

Notes